The World in the Twentieth Century

THE SECOND WORLD WAR

Other Books in the Series

THE FIRST WORLD WAR
  Richard Musman

HITLER AND MUSSOLINI
  Richard Musman

THE ROAD TO WAR: 1918–39
  Edmund Gray

Other Books by Martin Gilbert

WINSTON CHURCHILL
(Clarendon Biographies)

RECENT HISTORY ATLAS

BRITISH HISTORY ATLAS

AMERICAN HISTORY ATLAS

JEWISH HISTORY ATLAS

FIRST WORLD WAR ATLAS

THE EUROPEAN POWERS, 1900–1945

THE ROOTS OF APPEASEMENT

THE APPEASERS

Books edited by Martin Gilbert

BRITAIN AND GERMANY
  BETWEEN THE WARS

PLOUGH MY OWN FURROW:
The Life of Lord Allen of Hurtwood

SERVANT OF INDIA

CENTURY OF CONFLICT
Essays for A. J. P. Taylor

The World in the Twentieth Century

THE
SECOND
WORLD WAR

MARTIN GILBERT

1970

CHATTO & WINDUS
LONDON

Published by
Chatto and Windus (Educational) Ltd
42 William IV Street
London W.C.2 .

Clarke, Irwin & Co. Ltd
Toronto

SBN 7010 0385 5

Printed in Great Britain by
Cox and Wyman Ltd
London, Fakenham and Reading

Contents

Table   *page*

1. The Human Cost of the Second World War   6
2. World Industrial Production in 1940   7
3. Main dates   7

Acknowledgements   10

Chapter

1. Hitler and the Coming of War   11
2. The German Conquest of Poland   18
3. The Russian Riddle   23
4. The War in the West   26
5. British Defiance   34
6. Italy Strikes   43
7. The United States and the War   47
8. The Growing Storm   50
9. Russia under Attack   55
10. Russia at War   58
11. Japan   64
12. Global War   72
13. Behind Enemy Lines   76
14. Roads to Victory: The Pacific   82
15. Roads to Victory: Europe   87
16. War and Peace   99

For Further Reading   103

Index   105

The Human Cost of the Second World War

Russian soldiers killed in battle	5,500,000
Jews murdered in German concentration camps	5,500,000
German soldiers killed in battle	3,500,000
Polish civilians murdered by the Germans	3,000,000
Chinese military and civilian deaths	2,500,000
Russian prisoners-of-war murdered by the Germans	2,500,000
Russian civilians murdered by the Germans	2,000,000
European soldiers other than Germans or Russians killed in battle	2,000,000
Japanese soldiers killed in battle	1,500,000
Yugoslav civilians murdered by the Germans	1,300,000
Russian civilians died of starvation and bombardment in the siege of Leningrad	800,000
Austrian, Italian, Hungarian, Rumanian, Dutch, Belgian, Bulgarian and Finnish civilian dead	600,000
Japanese civilians killed in American bombing raids	550,000
German civilians killed in Anglo-American bombing raids	550,000
British and British Empire soldiers killed in battle	500,000
American soldiers killed in battle	300,000
Czech civilians murdered by the Germans	250,000
Greek civilians murdered by the Germans	140,000
British civilians killed in German air-raids	60,000

Total War Dead   approximately 33,000,000

Industrial Production in 1940

Illustrating the weakness of Germany when faced with the U.S.A., Russia and Britain combined. For comparative oil production see page 83.

Coal	Tons (millions)	Steel	Tons (millions)
U.S.A.	408	U.S.A	61
Britain	233	Russia	18
Russia	133	Britain	13
Germany	351 (against 774)	Germany	19 (against 92)

Iron	Tons (millions)	Manpower	Population (millions)
U.S.A.	43	Russia	192
Russia	15	U.S.A.	131
Britain	8	Britain	48
Germany	14 (against 66)	Germany	70 (against 371)

Main Dates

1939

Sept.	1	Germany invades Poland
Sept.	3	Britain and France declare war on Germany
Sept.	17	Russia invades Poland
Sept.	28	Russia and Germany partition Poland
Nov.	30	Russia invades Finland

1940

March	13	Finland makes peace with Russia
April	9	Germany invades Denmark and Norway
May	10	Germany invades Holland, Belgium and France
May	15	Holland surrenders
May	28	Belgium surrenders
June	22	France surrenders
Aug.	3	Italy invades British Somaliland
Aug.	8	The air 'Battle of Britain' begins over southern England

1940

Aug.	25	German date for invasion of Britain (later abandoned)
Sept.	7	German 'Blitz' bombing of British cities begins
Sept.	13	Italy invades Egypt
Oct.	7	Germany occupies Rumania
Dec.	11	Britain drives Italians from Egypt

1941

Feb.	9	Germany occupies Bulgaria
March	11	American Lend-Lease Act becomes law
April	5	Britain drives Italians from Abyssinia
April	6	Germany invades Yugoslavia and Greece
June	22	Germany invades Russia
July	7	U.S.A. occupies Iceland, Japan occupies Saigon
Aug.	9	First meeting of Churchill and Roosevelt at sea off Newfoundland
Aug.	21	Germans surround Leningrad; siege continues for over three years, 800,000 Russians killed
Sept.	1	Britain and Russia occupy Persia
Dec.	5	German armies fail to enter Moscow
Dec.	7	Japan attacks U.S. naval base at Pearl Harbor
Dec.	8	Japan occupies Siam and attacks Malaya
Dec.	10	Germany declares war on the United States
Dec.	25	Japan occupies Hong Kong

1942

Jan.	1	United Nations Declaration signed by twenty-six nations in Washington
Jan.	2	Japan invades Philippines
Feb.	8	Japan invades Burma
June	6	Japan fails to conquer Midway Island
June	10	Germans kill 172 men and boys at Lidice, Czechoslovakia as reprisal
July	1	Germany invades Egypt
Nov.	3	Britain drives German forces from Egypt

1943

Feb.	2	German army surrenders at Stalingrad
April	18	The Jews of Warsaw revolt against the Germans
May	13	German and Italian armies in North Africa surrender
May	30	Germans suppress Jewish revolt in Warsaw and murder all survivors

1943

Aug.	7	Allies conquer Sicily
Sept.	3	Allies invade Italy
Nov.	27	Churchill, Roosevelt, and Stalin meet at Teheran

1944

April	2	German armies driven out of Russia
June	4	Allies enter Rome
June	6	Allies land in Normandy
June	10	Germans kill all 642 inhabitants of Oradour-sur-Glane, France, as reprisal
Aug.	1	Polish rising against the Germans in Warsaw
Aug.	25	Allies enter Paris
Oct.	20	U.S. forces begin reconquest of Philippines
Oct.	23	U.S. fleet defeats Japanese at Leyte Gulf

1945

Feb.	3	Churchill, Roosevelt and Stalin meet at Yalta
Feb.	13	Russians enter Budapest
Feb.	13	Anglo-American air-raid in Dresden kills over 40,000 Germans
March	7	U.S. forces cross the Rhine at Remagen
March	9	U.S. air-raid on Tokyo kills over 80,000 Japanese
March	25	U.S. forces capture Iwo Jima Island
April	13	Russians enter Vienna
April	26	Russian and U.S. troops link up in Germany
May	2	Berlin surrenders to Russian forces
May	8	All German forces in Europe surrender
June	21	U.S. forces capture Okinawa
July	15	Churchill, Truman and Stalin meet at Potsdam
Aug.	6	First atom bomb dropped on Hiroshima: 80,000 killed
Aug.	8	Russia invades Japan
Aug.	9	Second atom bomb dropped on Nagasaki: 40,000 killed
Aug.	14	Japan surrenders

Acknowledgements

The author and publishers are grateful to Rebecca West for permission to quote from pp. 45–6 of *Black Lamb and Grey Falcon* published by Macmillan.

The sources for the photographs are as follows:
Associated Press, 16, 21, 23, 26; Paul Popper, 27; Radio Times Hulton Picture Library, 5, 10; Dr. A. Ben Bernfes, 22; Suddeutscher Verlag, Munich, 1, 3; Imperial War Museum, 20, 28; Bundesarchiv, Bonn, 8; Fox Photographs, 6; Wide World Photographs, 9; Ralph Martin, 19, 24, 30, 31; Erich Andres, Hamburg, 29; Mirror Pic, 11; Alexander Werth, 15; Randall Gould, 17. Unfortunately we have not in all cases been able to trace the copyright owners of the photographs used in this book.

1

Hitler and the Coming of War

I N January 1933 Adolf Hitler became Chancellor of Germany. It was a turning point in the history of the world. Hitler's aim was to make Germany the most powerful nation in Europe. Fifteen years had passed since the German Empire was defeated in the First World War.

Under the Treaty of Versailles, which it had signed in 1919, Germany was forbidden to build up a large army again. Strict limits were placed on the number of ships and planes which it could build. Its colonies were taken away by Britain and the other victorious powers. It had to pay the victor powers large sums of money as reparation for the damage done by its armies during the war. The German people were not accustomed to defeat. Proud, industrious and highly disciplined, they felt humiliated by their failure to defeat France, Britain and the United States. In 1933 Adolf Hitler seemed to offer them new hope and a brighter future. He promised jobs for those without work, industry for the factory owners, pride for the patriots.

Most of the Germans who supported Hitler when he came to power did not want to make war on other countries. They were not a bloodthirsty people. Some of the finest music and the most moving literature came from their country. Many of the greatest advances in medicine and science were of German origin. But when Hitler appealed to their sense of national pride, he quickly excited and unbalanced them. He made them believe that Germany would only be respected abroad if it were strong in military power. The majority of Germans forgot that a nation is respected, not by the size of its bombs, but by its way of life, and by its contribution to the general well-being of mankind. Under Hitler's leadership the Germans seemed to forget that it was their cultural achievements and their industry which had made them great. They turned instead to the dangerous search for the military mastery of Europe.

Hitler ruled Germany for six years of peace and five of war. His boast was that he would create a new German Empire to last for a thousand years. His actual achievement was to destroy the dominance of Germany among the powers of the world, and to reduce Germany to the status of a second-class power. The Germans put their trust in a man who promised them national glory. But he brought them instead the physical ruin and division of their country, as well as the hatred of the other peoples of Europe by whom they had wanted to be praised. The offer of power and glory unbalanced the German people. In the first six years of peace they were too excited by what Hitler promised them to see the dangers that lay ahead.

Hitler's intentions appeared honourable. He brought flourishing industry, work for all, fast trains, fine roads (the first motorways in Europe), and all the outward signs of a rich, prosperous and expanding nation. But his methods were odious. From the moment that he came to power he set about destroying the parliamentary system upon which German democracy was based. He imprisoned any political opponents who dared to criticize him. His secret police, the Gestapo, made people afraid to speak their minds. By 1935 Germany had become a police state.

Hitler's greatest cruelty was reserved for the Jewish people. It

April 1933: German Communists in one of Hitler's detention camps for political prisoners, Oranienburg, near Berlin.

was his treatment of the Jews of Germany which showed the outside world what Hitler and the new Germany really represented. In 1933 there were over half a million German Jews. Most of them were almost completely assimilated to the German way of life. It was often impossible to pick them out from the mass of Germans. Many Jews had fought bravely in the German armies during the First World War. They loved Germany intensely. Indeed, it was German Jews who had made many of the greatest scientific and medical discoveries. In every sphere of German life where they were active, the Jews enriched German culture.

Hitler made it his mission to drive the Jews entirely out of German life. He succeeded in doing so. But the cost for Germany was a high one. Hitler's cruel treatment of the Jews cut Germany off, perhaps for ever, from one of the richest and most constructive sources of German genius. Jewish children were not allowed to mix with their fellow German children at school. By 1939 the Jews were forbidden to practise as doctors or lawyers. Many towns expelled them altogether. Their synagogues were burned down. Their shops were boycotted. Their daily life filled with fear for the future.

Many of Germany's neighbours did not like the way Hitler behaved within his country. His brutal methods towards political opponents, Jews and all who spoke out against him, seemed more akin to superstitious and barbaric medieval behaviour than to a way of life fit for the twentieth century. Many Englishmen had felt sympathy for the defeated Germans. They had wanted to help put Germany on its feet again. But now they began to have serious doubts about the future. Only a few months after Hitler came to power in 1933 Jews had been savagely beaten up in the streets of Berlin. 'The German atrocities,' wrote Lady Violet Bonham Carter, daughter of a former British Liberal Prime Minister, 'make me feel quite ill with rage and shame. They also make me feel foolish at having been so steadfast a pro-German ever since they became under-dogs.'

Austen Chamberlain, who in 1925 had been in charge of British Foreign Policy and was a leading advocate of reconciliation with Germany, asked bluntly in the House of Commons in 1933: 'What is this new spirit of German nationalism? It is the worst of the all-Prussian Imperialism, with an added savagery, a racial pride, an exclusiveness which cannot allow to any fellow-subject not of "pure Nordic birth" equality of rights and citizenship within the nation to which he belongs. . . . Germany is afflicted by this narrow, exclusive, aggressive spirit, by which it is a crime to be in favour of peace and a crime to be a Jew. This is not a Germany to which we can afford to make concessions.'

Hitler was not content to discipline the Germans. He was not content to turn them more and more into a docile mass without thoughts or words of its own. He was not content to see his National Socialist, or 'Nazi' party, spy and pry into every corner of German privacy. He was not content to drive the Jews out of German life. He wanted Germany to expand. He wanted the German armies, which he was secretly building up, to conquer new territory. He wanted to make as many countries as possible fear and obey him.

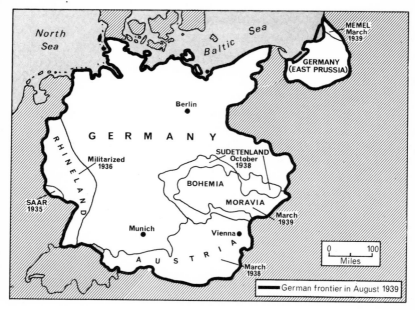

German Peacetime Expansion, 1935–1939

By 1939 Hitler had extended Germany's frontiers to include two previously independent states, Austria and Czechoslovakia. He did this by a combination of violent threats and clever promises. The other nations of Europe felt powerless to stop him. They were unwilling to pit their combined armed strength against him. Some people thought they might have halted his advances had they united to challenge him. But each nation watched while Hitler threatened someone else. Few people seemed to think that they themselves might one day be threatened by his growing strength and mounting ambition. A few, lonely voices in Europe and the United States warned that there was a great danger in letting Hitler have his way in central Europe. But the general view was that Hitler would never threaten Britain, France or America.

The western powers disliked the way Hitler conquered the little nations of central Europe. But they pretended that Hitler's ambitions were limited to these small countries, and did little to defend themselves or to build up a strong alliance of democratic states. One person who saw clearly that there was probably little limit to Hitler's ambition was Winston Churchill. He spoke often in the House of Commons and over the wireless, warning the peoples of Europe and the United States that Hitler meant to harm them. But they did not want to listen to his warnings. They preferred to believe those who told them that Hitler would soon soften his demands and become a peace-loving, quiet, sensible statesman to whom they could all turn without fear, and indeed to mutual advantage. Looking back over this period Churchill later asked: 'What is the explanation of the enslavement of Europe by the German Nazi regime? How did they do it? It is but a few years ago since one united gesture by the peoples, great and small, who are now broken in the dust, would have warded off from mankind the fearful ordeal it has had to undergo. But there was no unity. There was no vision. The nations were pulled down one by one while the others gaped and chattered. One by one, each in his turn, they let themselves be caught. One after another they were felled by brutal violence or poisoned from within by subtle intrigue.'

In August 1939 Hitler demanded yet another extension of the German frontier. This time he turned his eyes upon Poland, a country of thirty million people set between Germany and Russia. Hitler had signed a treaty of friendship with Russia. But he knew that if he wished to dominate Europe, it was Russia he must defeat. And it was across Poland that his armies must march if they were to reach the vast plains of Russia.

Hitler's threats against Poland were as violent as those against Austria and Czechoslovakia had been. But now both Britain and France became alarmed. They promised that if Hitler attacked Poland they would come to Poland's defence. At last it was clear

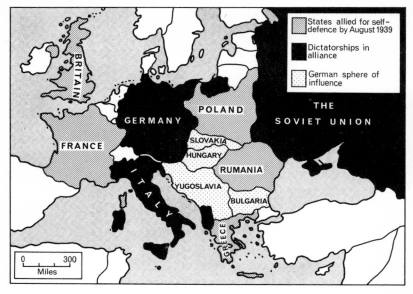

European Alliances, August 1939

that the western democracies were prepared to defend a country that was in danger. At last they saw that a threat to any one of Hitler's victims was a threat to them all.

Europe was now starkly divided. On the one hand were those countries where the rights of individuals meant little. In these countries government was carried on by means of terror. These countries hoped to expand their territory, if necessary by war. They wanted to dominate their neighbours. They were ruled, not by parliaments or elected ministers, but by dictators. Hitler in Germany, Stalin in Russia and Mussolini in Italy, were now linked together, willing to strike at neighbouring countries. They were not interested in the reluctance of ordinary people in their country to begin a second war after only twenty years of uneasy peace. The dictator countries of Europe also had a friend in the Far East, Hirohito, the emperor of Japan. The Japanese military chiefs had pushed Hirohito forward to a position where the Japanese, like the Russians, Italians and Germans, were taught to despise their neighbours, and to regard war as a good and noble thing. The Japanese had already invaded China. Since 1937 their armies and their bombs had brought bloodshed, poverty and chaos to vast areas of the Chinese mainland.

These four dictator states hoped to build their power and extend their territory by military means. Confronting them were those countries which still respected the rights of the individual, and had no desire to conquer others. These democratic states were not always united in knowing how they should act against the threat of the dictators. But they were convinced that tyranny, conquest, the persecution of Jews, the imprisonment of political critics, press censorship and all the other forms of dictatorial life were evil. Their beliefs were later expressed most clearly by the President of the United States, Franklin D. Roosevelt, who said, 'We look forward to a world founded upon four essential human freedoms. The first is freedom of speech and expression—everywhere in the world. The second is freedom of every person to worship God in his own way—everywhere in the world. The third is freedom from want—which, translated into world terms, means economic understandings which will secure to every nation a healthy peace-time life for its inhabitants—everywhere in the world. The fourth is freedom from fear—which, translated into world terms, means a world-wide reduction of armaments to such a point and in such a thorough fashion that no nation will be in a position to commit an act of physical aggression against any neighbour—anywhere in the world.'

On 1 September 1939 the German army invaded Poland. Hitler's aim was swift and total conquest. Two days later Britain and France honoured their promise to Poland and declared war against him. The United States remained outside the conflict. But President Roosevelt made it quite clear that his sympathies lay entirely with the democracies.

Britain and France were not only at war with Germany for the defence of one small nation, Poland, against a large and aggressive neighbour. They were at war because they now saw that the Nazi system would destroy them and their way of life unless it could be defeated. They were fighting for those same four freedoms on which Roosevelt said that democracy was based.

The war against Hitler was a war against brutality. It was a war which Hitler alone had sought. If the Nazi system were to triumph in Europe Hitler would have to win that war. By extending Nazi rule over the Continent, and perhaps later over Russia as well, Hitler aimed at reducing daily life to a pattern of uncritical obedi-ence to Germany. He wanted people to be afraid to speak against his actions. He was now determined to destroy the liberties of all those he disliked. Not only the Jews in Europe, but Christians also; Socialists, Communists, Liberals, and anyone with a critical mind, all would be rooted out. They would be brutally treated and perhaps even killed in one of the many 'concentration camps' which Hitler had, from 1933, set up as prisons for his political opponents.

Winston Churchill, who had been brought into the British Government on the outbreak of war, told the House of Commons that the war was not a question of fighting only for Poland. The issue was a much wider one, he said: 'We are fighting to save the whole world from the pestilence of Nazi tyranny and in defence of all that is most sacred to man. This is no war of domination or imperial aggrandizement or material gain; no war to shut any country out of its sunlight or means of progress. It is a war, viewed in its inherent quality, to establish, on impregnable rocks, the rights of the individual, and it is a war to establish and revive the stature of man.'

2

The German Conquest of Poland

THE Germans launched their attack on Poland shortly before dawn on 1 September 1939. Although the Polish troops fought bravely, they were unable to halt the German advance. The German army had been trained for some years for just such a war. Their main strength lay in the number of small tanks and armoured cars. These could cross rough country quickly. They enabled the Germans to sweep forward, and penetrate deep into Poland. In advance of these armoured columns, German planes bombed the Polish roads and railways, causing chaos to the Polish defences. They also bombed Polish cities. In this way they spread fear and confusion to the civilian population far behind the front line. This was the technique of the *Blitzkrieg*, or lightening war. The *Blitzkrieg* was the most frightening and the most effective of all Hitler's military techniques.

The Poles defended themselves bravely. But their geographic

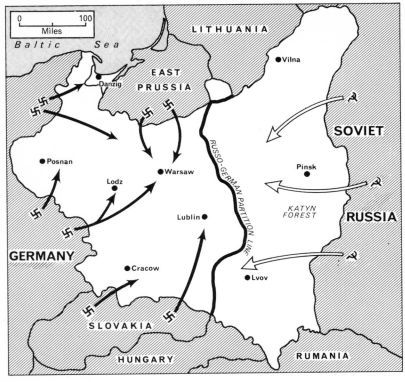

The Conquest of Poland, September 1939

position was indefensible. The Germans were able to attack simultaneously from the north, the west and the south. The German armies quickly pressed in towards Russia. But two weeks before war began Hitler had signed a special agreement with Russia, under which the Russians could occupy the eastern part of Poland if Germany conquered the rest. Thus it was that the Russians advanced into Poland only two weeks after the German invasion had begun, but when most of the Polish cities were over-run and the Polish army in retreat. Russian soldiers moved rapidly through the eastern part of Poland until they linked up with the German armies. The Polish escape routes were cut off. Thousands of Polish officers turned to the advancing Russians and asked for asylum from the Germans. The Russians agreed to give these brave men a place of refuge. Two years later many of them were found dead in a mass grave in the Katyn forest. They had been murdered by the very Russians who had offered to help them.

When the Germans began their attack on Poland, the Polish Government asked Britain and France, its two western allies, for help. But neither had prepared any plans for sending help to Poland. Both were anxious to do what they could to enable Poland to preserve its independence. But they had no desire to launch an attack on Germany in the west. Such an attack might have forced many of the German troops then invading Poland to be hurried back to defend the Rhine. But neither Britain nor France felt strong enough to do anything so bold. The German General, Jodl, claimed after the war: 'If we did not collapse in 1939, that was due only to the fact that during the Polish campaign the British and French defences were completely inactive.'

The Poles begged the British to bomb Germany. They argued that if the Germans felt threatened by British bombers they would be forced to recall many of their own planes from Poland, where they were causing so much chaos. But the British were afraid to bomb Germany. They believed that if they did so, the Germans would bomb them in return. Neither Britain nor France seemed willing to be drawn into a full-scale war with Germany. Although they had declared war on Hitler, they still needed time to prepare their defences, which the pre-war Governments had left weak and incomplete.

In mid-September however, spurred on by Polish pressure, the British began a curious form of warfare. They sent planes over Germany, filled, not with bombs, but with leaflets. The Royal Air Force dropped millions of these leaflets over Germany. They fluttered down into the streets, parks and gardens of twenty cities. Those Germans who bothered to look at the leaflets found themselves reading an account of how wicked they had been to attack Poland, and how wrong they were to support Hitler. Leaflet bombing was not a success. It certainly failed to help the Poles. By the end of September the German and Russian armies had come together and Polish resistance was at an end.

Sixty-six thousand Poles were killed during this first month of war. The British continued to drop leaflets over Germany. The Germans were elated by their swift and total victory. It seemed to many of them to be a clear proof of Hitler's genius that in one month he could conquer a country of thirty million people, allied with two powerful western states, and rich in coal, steel and agriculture.

October 1940: Hitler takes the salute as German troops parade through conquered Warsaw.

The British and French were shocked by Hitler's rapid success. They were also frightened by the pictures which they saw of the destruction of Warsaw by German bombs. It was clear that the Germans had now mastered the technique of the *Blitzkrieg*. They could overrun vast areas with little difficulty. People in the west were stunned to see Poland, which looked so large on the map of Europe, eaten up so quickly by the German and Russian armies. Churchill tried bravely to raise people's spirits when he broadcast to the British people: 'Poland has again been overrun by two of the great powers which held her in bondage for a hundred and fifty years but were unable to quench the spirit of the Polish nation . . . the soul of Poland is indestructible. . . . She will rise again like a rock, which may for a time be submerged by a tidal wave, but which remains a rock.'

For the British, the Polish spirit was something which they could now admire and praise. But for the Germans it was something to be broken and destroyed. From the moment of their conquest, the Germans treated the Poles with the utmost brutality. They immediately set up a rule of terror which lasted for five years. Any Pole who criticized Germany was shot. Many university profes-

German S.S. troops march away Polish peasants

sors, writers, journalists, politicians and leading citizens were put to death. By the end of the war over three million Poles had been killed. There was nothing glorious or romantic about the war in the east. The Germans sent hundreds of thousands of Poles to work in German factories. They took all the mineral wealth of Poland which they needed. They pillaged its farms. They terrorized its people. They spread fear, misery and death through Poland on a scale unknown to modern Europe.

1942: seven Polish civilians are hanged publicly by the Germans, who announced officially that for every German shot they would kill one hundred Poles as reprisals.

In the west people waited to see where Hitler would move next. There were some in England and France who hoped that he would soon agree to make peace. As a result of his conquest of Poland, he was now master of central Europe. He ruled more territory than Germany had ever ruled before in its short history as a united country. He had brought together all German speaking people within one frontier. He had conquered the wealth and gained the manpower of three independent states, Austria, Czechoslovakia and Poland. This, surely, was all he could want?

It is probable that Hitler himself did not know what to do next. He actually offered to make peace with Britain. But his offer was turned down. It would have meant accepting the German conquest of Poland, and all that the Germans were doing there. Hitler waited, uncertain of where to strike or whether to strike at all. The British and French also waited. They were glad that no German bombs were falling on their cities. They did not intend to provoke them. The 'phoney' war had begun. It lasted all winter and all spring.

3

The Russian Riddle

FOR seven months, from October 1939 to April 1940, Britain and France watched and waited. News filtered out from Poland of terrible German brutality against the Polish people. It seemed that there was nothing that could be done but to sit nervously wondering whether Hitler would strike again. Although western Europe was still unconquered and unattacked, its people lived in constant fear. They busily prepared themselves for an invasion which could come at any time and from almost any direction. The Germans ruled central Europe by conquest and dominated western Europe by fear.

Of all the European powers, Germany was now the strongest and the largest. Many people, both in Germany and outside it, felt that whenever the Germans wished to conquer, they could do so with little difficulty. But there was one country whose strength was less well known. This was Russia. Since the Bolshevik Revolution of 1917 Russia had stood outside Europe, isolated and without friends. No one knew the strength of its armies. No one could tell how courageous its leader, Joseph Stalin, would be once danger threatened. Hitler had wisely come to an agreement with Russia before his invasion of Poland. This 'Nazi-Soviet Pact' had made them partners in conquest. By giving Russia the eastern part of Poland, Hitler bought Russian friendship. But no one knew how long this vast Communist country would be willing to remain the partner of Nazi Germany.

Many Russians feared that Hitler's ambition was to conquer Russia. They sensed that he wanted to control the rich grainland of the Ukraine and the oil wells of the Caucasus. They realized that he regarded the Russian people as he regarded the Jews, with contempt and hatred. Like the Poles, the Russians were a Slav people. Throughout their history they had defended themselves against German attack. What was happening in Poland should have warned them of what could easily happen in Russia also, once Hitler decided to attack.

The Russian occupation of eastern Poland was not entirely motivated by greed. The Russians were trying to set up as wide a barrier as possible between themselves and Germany. Many people in England were most bitter to see Stalin make common cause with Hitler. It seemed to them that there was now no difference between the Fascist and Communist dictators. But Churchill, who had always been an outspoken critic of Communism, realized that Russia's action had another motive, which perhaps boded well for Britain. 'Russia,' he said, 'has pursued a cold policy of self-interest. We could have wished that the Russian armies should be standing on their present lines as the friends and allies of Poland, instead of as invaders. But that the Russian armies should stand on this line, was clearly necessary for the safety of Russia against the Nazi menace. At any rate, the line is there, and an eastern front has been created which Nazi Germany does not dare assail. . . . I cannot forecast to you the action of Russia. It is a riddle wrapped in a mystery inside an enigma; but perhaps there is a key. The key is Russian national interest.'

The Russians had created a defensive barrier in Poland which, they hoped, would serve as a protection against any German attack. Farther north, they looked nervously at their frontier with Finland. This frontier came very near to the city of Leningrad. If Finland were to be controlled by Germany it would certainly threaten the security of Leningrad, and of all northern Russia. Stalin therefore decided to annex part of Finland. His aim was to build a deeper defensive corridor along the Russian frontier. But the Finns were not willing to give up their territory under threat of attack. Like the Poles, they had become fully independent only twenty years before. They prized their independence. The Russians had ruled Finland for over two hundred years. The Finns did not wish to see Russia back again, even if it were limited to frontier districts.

The Russians were unable to persuade the Finns to hand over the border territory. In anger, they invaded Finland. The second campaign of the war had begun. The Finns resisted for several months. The outside world was amazed that such a small nation could successfully resist the great Russia.

Britain and France decided to send arms and planes to help the Finns. They felt ashamed at having done so little for Poland two months before. But by the time their aid was ready, Finland had surrendered. The Finnish Government agreed to hand over the border territories Stalin demanded. The Commander-in-Chief of the Finnish army, Marshal Mannerheim, announced the Finnish surrender: 'After hard fighting lasting more than a hundred days, Finland has concluded peace. United and ready for all sacrifices, our people took up arms to protect what they treasured more than life: honour, liberty and western civilization. Now we have to cede parts of our beloved Fatherland to superior forces; our villages and cities have been burnt down and devastated. But with undismayed courage, heads erect, we are still standing, protected by our army, worn out in many battles, but not defeated in spite of the enormously superior forces of the enemy.'

It was March 1940. Only the dictator powers had so far been successful, after six months of war. America remained neutral; alert but aloof, sympathetic to the democracies but unwilling to plunge into war. In the Far East, now almost unnoticed by the Europeans, Japan continued to advance through China, bombing, systematically destroying, and subjugating the Chinese people. In England and France fear was giving way to boredom. The 'phoney' war became more and more like peace. The German danger seemed less and less real as spring approached.

4

The War in the West

In April 1940 the British leaders at last decided to take bold action. They knew that, as part of the war effort, the Germans were carrying iron ore by ship from Norway to Germany. This ore was used to make German weapons. The British therefore planned to close this sea route by laying mines along the coast of Norway. But the British decision to take the initiative came too late. For on the same day that British destroyers began to drop their mines, the Germans themselves attacked northwards. Their aim was to conquer Denmark and Norway. Thereby they would control the whole Scandinavian coast from the Baltic Sea to the Arctic Ocean.

The British and German forces thus found themselves thrown face to face quite by accident. The British were outnumbered. The Germans advanced rapidly northwards. Denmark was conquered in a single day. After a month of fierce fighting the British troops were driven almost entirely out of Norway. The Germans won control both of the sea route and of the great Norwegian land mass. Once again the German method of bombing towns and advancing with superior mechanized forces was successful. Once again, after only a month of fighting, the Germans could point to another vast area of Europe, comprising two proud and independent states, subjugated to German rule.

The people of Britain were deeply shocked. How was it, they asked, that their decision to be more active in the war should have met with such a sudden and complete setback? How was it that after six months of war British plans should prove so poor and British power so thin? Many people felt that the Prime Minister, Neville Chamberlain, ought to resign, and his Conservative Government be replaced by a Coalition Government of all political parties. The need was for the best men in the most important positions. Party politics seemed irrelevant in war time.

News was published in the British newspapers in April of further German brutality in Poland. The Germans were killing Catholic priests and Jewish rabbis. They even forced some of them to dig their own graves before they were shot. The Pope himself gave publicity to these German outrages. British consciences were

Finland and Norway, 1939

roused by the crudity and barbarism of the German behaviour
in the east. After all, it was on Poland's behalf that they had gone to
war six months before. In the spring of 1940 Polish suffering led to
a rapidly growing hatred of German actions. The British were
alarmed. Not only did Poland, Britain's eastern ally, lie prostrate
and powerless, suffering great agony; but now Norway and Denmark had fallen under German rule. No one could tell how cruel
would be the fate of their priests and politicians, their writers and
doctors, their lawyers and artists. In German-occupied Europe
even the man in the street, minding his own business, anxious only
to earn enough money to keep his home and family together, was
not safe against Nazi tyranny.

The British people felt that they needed more dynamic leadership. It was clear that they must act with greater speed and skill
than they had done so far, if they were to avoid the fate of Austria,
Czechoslovakia, Poland, Norway and Denmark.

On 6 May 1940 the British newspapers began a strong attack on
the weaknesses of Chamberlain and his Government. On 7 and 8
May the British Parliament debated the failure of the war in Norway. It was a bitter debate. While Chamberlain himself was
speaking there were frequent, angry, interruptions. Members of
Parliament of all parties demanded Chamberlain's resignation.
'War is not won by shirking risks,' said Leo Amery, a Conservative
Member of Parliament and former Cabinet Minister: 'We cannot
go on as we are. There must be a change. . . . As long as the present
methods prevail, all our resources are not going to see us through.'
David Lloyd George, who had been Prime Minister in the last
two years of the First World War, declared passionately that there
was nothing that could contribute more to victory than that
Chamberlain should resign.

While the British people worried over their lack of success, and
the British Parliament debated with mounting anguish the failures
and weaknesses of its politicians, Adolf Hitler struck again. On
10 May German bombs fell on the cities of Belgium, Holland and
Luxembourg. German tanks swept with unexpected speed past
the frontiers of these three ill-prepared and ill-defended states.
Neither Belgium, Luxembourg nor Holland had expected a
German attack, any more than Denmark had a month before.
They were small countries which only wanted to be left alone.
But Hitler was not interested in respecting their neutrality. He
wished to make himself the master of western Europe in the same

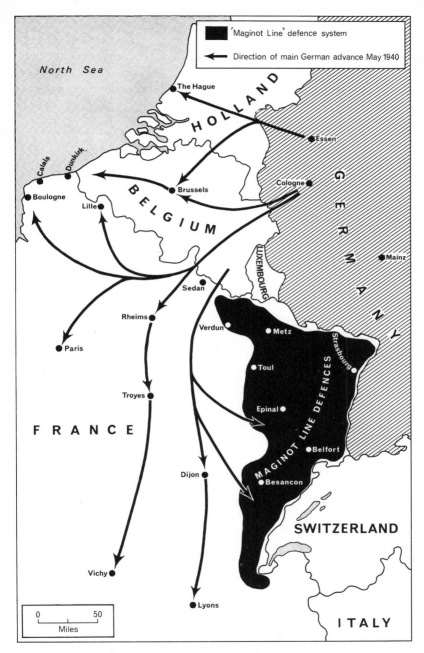

The German Advance, May 1940

way that he had already, in under two years, made himself master of central Europe and Scandinavia. Hitler's greatest asset was the speed with which he acted. He was always one step ahead of those he wished to conquer. He struck without warning, catching each of his victims by surprise.

On the same day that he attacked Belgium and Holland, Hitler launched the third German invasion of France in fifty years. The French had built a wide belt of defensive forts and underground strongpoints stretching from the Belgian frontier to Switzerland. These massive fortifications were secure. The Germans knew that they could not break them easily. The French had sat behind this 'Maginot line' throughout the phoney war. They had little fear of a German attack. But the German army ignored the French fortifications. It attacked through Belgium, thus by-passing the Maginot line entirely. The Germans therefore broke into France where it was least defended. Many Frenchmen were thrown into a mood of gloom and despondency. Were they once again, for the third time, to suffer all the heartbreak of a war fought across French fields and through French towns? Were they once again, as in 1914, to see the armies of many nations fighting over their countryside, destroying their crops, cattle and farms, and devastating their villages and towns?

May 1940: refugees fleeing before the German invasion in the north of France.

Some Frenchmen felt that the best course would be to surrender. But the French Government, led by Paul Reynaud, decided to resist. The odds against them were high. They were no better able to defeat the combination of German bombs and tanks than the Poles or the Norwegians had been. But all the pluck and pugnacity of the French people came to the fore in the five weeks of French resistance. Those who wished to fight on, despite the heavy odds against them, did so bravely, tenaciously, but with dwindling hopes. Those who wished to surrender sat solemn and silent, waiting for the moment when they could push Reynaud aside and make peace with Germany.

On the very day of the German invasion into France, Belgium and Holland, the British Prime Minister, Neville Chamberlain, resigned. He was succeeded by Winston Churchill, who formed a Coalition Government made up of the three political parties, Conservative, Labour and Liberal. Churchill, like Reynaud in France, was determined to resist the Germans to the very end. He too was faced by a small number of his fellow-countrymen who felt that the best course lay in making peace with Hitler while there was yet time, before the Germans invaded England. These people felt that if Britain accepted Germany's conquests in Europe, Hitler would agree to leave Britain and the British Empire alone. Churchill refused to accept such speculation. He told the Members of his Government, and the people of Britain, that he would never make peace with Hitler. 'I have nothing to offer,' he told the House of Commons, 'but blood, toil, tears and sweat. You ask, what is our policy? I will say: It is to wage war by sea, land and air, with all our might and with all the strength that God can give us; to wage war against a monstrous tyranny, never surpassed in the dark, lamentable catalogue of human crime. That is our policy. You ask, what is our aim? I answer in one word —*victory*: victory at all costs, victory in spite of all terror, victory, however long and hard the road may be, for without victory there is no survival.'

Churchill spoke many times to the British people over the radio. These broadcasts played a large part in convincing the people that Britain should try to resist Germany, even if it meant fighting the Germans in England. Churchill's Government acted with speed and decision. A large number of British troops were fighting side by side with the French and Belgians. British pilots did their utmost to weaken German air-mastery over France. British sup-

plies helped bolster the French war effort. But all these activities
were in vain. The Germans were elated by their success in
northern and eastern Europe. They were well-armed, well-
equipped and highly mechanized. Swiftly and confidently they
pushed forward into Belgium, Holland and France. The Dutch,
their cities badly bombed, their small country appalled by the
heavy casualties, surrendered on 15 May. The Belgian Government, equally horrified at the speed of the German advance and
all the damage which the Germans were doing, surrendered on
28 May, after a brave and costly resistance.

In less than a month after the German attack, the British troops
in France, over two hundred and fifty thousand in all, were driven
back to the beaches of Dunkirk. Here they were surrounded by
German troops. Cut off from any chance of help, cramped into
a small stretch of coast, under constant German bombardment
from the air, they looked anxiously across the channel. And then
the 'miracle' of Dunkirk took place. As many ships as could sail,
destroyers, pleasure boats, motor launches from the seaside
resorts of the south coast of England, ferried back and forward
across the Channel carrying these soldiers away to safety.

June 1940: in seven days 300,000 British and French troops escaped from the
    beaches of Dunkirk to Britain. Many were killed waiting for ships to take them
    away. To protect themselves the troops used their rifles to shoot at German
    planes.

June 1940: German soldiers march through Paris. In 1944 a German general refused to obey Hitler's order to burn Paris to the ground.

Within a week 190,000 English and 140,000 French soldiers had been rescued from the beaches. The British people were amazed that so many men had been saved from so desperate a situation. Ten days later the Germans entered Paris. On 22 June, only six weeks after the start of the German invasion, the French Government surrendered. Hitler was now master of western Europe.

Defeat brought humiliation for the people of France. The Germans occupied the north and west, including the capital,

Paris, and the industrial centres near the Belgian and German frontiers. Hitler allowed the southern half of France to remain under direct French control, but this 'puppet' regime acted largely as he wished. It imprisoned his enemies and helped his policies. It was known, after its centre of government, as 'Vichy' France, and was ruled by a hero of the First World War, Marshal Pétain, who felt that France could only survive if it bent to German will. Other Frenchmen felt differently. Another soldier, Charles de Gaulle, refused to believe that France must submit. He immediately set up a 'Free French' army in England, and from his active exile was able to increase French resistance both inside and outside France.

Defiantly, de Gaulle broadcast over the British radio from London to the conquered French people, many of whom were later to cheer his courage and follow his banner. 'Has the last word been said? Has all hope gone? Is defeat final? No! Believe me, and I know what I am talking about, when I say that France is not lost. . . . For France does not stand alone. . . . She can make a solid block with the British Empire, which has command of the seas and continues the struggle. She can, like England, make limitless use of the huge industrial resources of the United States. . . . Whatever may happen, the flame of French resistance *must* not go out, and *will* not go out.'

5

British Defiance

THROUGHOUT the later summer of 1940 the British waited for Hitler's invasion. From the cliffs of Dover they watched anxiously across the twenty-one miles of water which separated them from Nazi-dominated Europe. On every southern beach they laid sprawling coils of barbed wire in which to tangle and trap an invading force. Along river valleys they built squat pill-boxes from which to shoot at any advancing troops. On hills and high buildings they placed anti-aircraft guns with which to bring down attacking aircraft. Above most towns rose into the air elephant-like barrage balloons, to prevent enemy aircraft flying too low. In each village, units of the 'Home Guard', mostly men too old for military service, drilled with rifles and even broomsticks, and worked out what they would do if well-armed, well-trained German soldiers were to appear on the borders of their parish.

The strongest fear in Britain was of a German parachute invasion. In order to prevent enemy paratroopers from finding out where they had landed, all road signs and station names were painted out. At night, black-out restrictions were strictly enforced. Every window had to be covered so carefully that from the air no city would stand out as a target for German bombers. Car head-lamps and traffic lights were transformed by tape and paint into tiny slits of light. Even the Belisha Beacons, which had been in operation for only a few years, were turned off. At night, Britain was plunged into a man-made darkness.

Everyone seemed certain that the Germans would invade. The Government distributed millions of leaflets which told people what to do in the event of attack. To the frequent question 'What do I do if fighting breaks out in my neighbourhood?' the leaflet's answer was: 'Keep indoors or in your shelter until the battle is over. If you can have a trench in your garden or field, so much the better. You may want to use it for protection if your house is damaged. But if you are at work, or if you have special orders, carry on as long as possible and only take cover when danger approaches. If you are on your way to work, finish your journey if you can. If you see an enemy tank, or a few enemy soldiers, do not assume that the enemy are in control of the area. What you have seen may be a party sent on in advance or stragglers from the main body who can easily be rounded up.' Such optimistic advice did little to calm those who were afraid. But Churchill continued to broadcast with his unique and effective mixture of facing-the-facts, pugnacity, and humour. 'We are awaiting the coming invasion,' he said, 'and so are the fishes.'

Hitler was convinced that he could conquer Britain. On 16 July he drew up his 'Directive no. 16', instructing his generals to plan the invasion. He chose the code name 'Sea Lion'. Details were at once prepared. Invasion maps were drawn. Occupation zones were worked out. A list of the names of the strongest critics of Nazism was compiled. They would be immediately arrested once German rule was established. Another list was made of

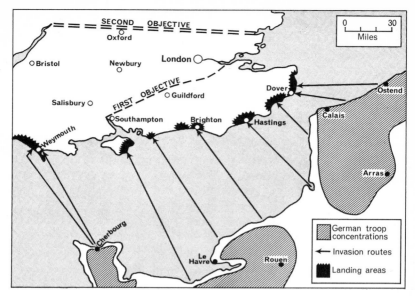

The Planned Invasion of England, July 1940

those who were thought to be friendly to Germany, and might therefore be willing to collaborate with the occupation forces. It was one of Hitler's pieces of fortune that in almost every country which he conquered, he found local people willing to help him impose his stern system. One of the first of these collaborators was Vidkun Quisling, a Norwegian army officer. He gave his name to all such 'quislings' who, from different motives, co-operated with their country's conquerors.

In the ports and river mouths of German-occupied Holland, Belgium and France, the Germans began to assemble a large armada of landing craft. German soldiers practised mock invasions on the beaches of northern Europe. Hitler fixed 25 August as a tentative invasion date.

In London, Churchill studied the mood of the British people. He saw and shared the fears of men and women in every walk of life. But he also knew the deep reserves of courage in his fellow-countrymen. During the First World War he had fought in the trenches of Flanders. He therefore knew what terrible hardships men would endure in a cause for which they believed. He had also seen, as Minister of Munitions in 1917, the exertions of which people were capable in factories, in order to provide the soldiers

Summer 1940: German soldiers practise for the invasion of Britain.

with weapons and munitions. He was convinced that the British would not give in easily to Germany.

Hitler may also have sensed the British mood. As the summer advanced he began to doubt whether an invasion would be as easy as he had earlier believed. He therefore decided to postpone the invasion. He decided instead to destroy Britain's air power. If he could do this, his invasion forces would be unmolested from the air. But the Royal Air Force was prepared. It had the advantage of a brilliant new invention, 'radar'. This made it possible to detect German planes before they reached the British coast. If they were flying high they could be spotted while still over France. Throughout the first year of the war scientists had been busy improving this radar detection system. Technicians set up a radar chain around the British coast which enabled German planes to be 'seen' on the radar screen in time for British fighters to get into the air and intercept them.

Throughout August the Germans attacked the British fighter

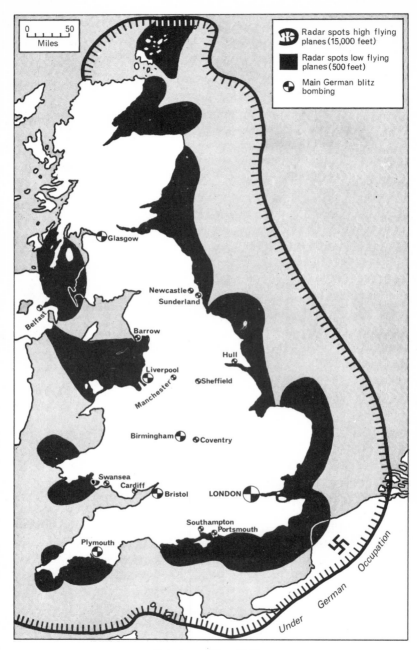

Scale: 0 — 50 Miles

Legend:
- Radar spots high flying planes (15,000 feet)
- Radar spots low flying planes (500 feet)
- Main German blitz bombing

Glasgow

Newcastle
Sunderland

Belfast

Barrow

Hull

Liverpool
Manchester
Sheffield

Birmingham
Coventry

Swansea
Cardiff
Bristol

LONDON

Southampton
Portsmouth

Plymouth

Under German Occupation

Britain at War, 1940

aircraft and their bases. Air battles took place over the farms and fields of southern England. People watched, mesmerized, as the sky filled with vapour trails and violence. One poet caught the mood of the onlookers in his description of two old ladies watching the air battle in Kent:

> 'Did they come over you again today?'
>   One lady asked another near the sea.
> 'Some came and some are down,' I heard her say
>   'And two are burning over by that tree,
> But won't you have another cup of tea?'

August 1940: during the Battle of Britain a German plane makes a forced landing in a British cornfield.

Slowly, but definitely, the British won control of their own skies. The air battle lasted a month. It was Hitler's first defeat of the war. It became known as the Battle of Britain. Of the pilots whose victory it was Churchill declared with pride, 'never in the field of human conflict was so much owed by so many to so few.'

Hitler failed to destroy British air power. British morale rose as a result of the victory. The chance of an easy German invasion had become remote. Hitler now turned to his final weapon, terror. His aim was to bomb the largest British cities so severely that the people would cry out for peace. He hoped that if he could reduce the major cities to rubble, Britain would surrender. His bombers had had this effect on the Dutch people. They had brought terror to Polish towns. Now they turned attention on Britain.

The first night of the 'blitz' was 7 September 1940, over London. For four months the German bombers dropped their bombs

1940: a London street after an air-raid. During the blitz as many as 10,000 fire bombs were dropped on London in one night.

10 May 1941: German bombs reduce the church of St. Clement Danes to a shell. Over fifty London churches were destroyed during the blitz and 60,000 civilians killed.

on the British cities. Each attack added to the death toll. Each morning saw the dazed survivors emerge from their shelters and survey the increasing area of devastation. Each night the radar reported on the increasing wave of bombers, and searchlights swept the sky trying to pinpoint the aerial invaders. The anti-aircraft gun crews waited, with little hope of being able to shoot down the high-flying bombers. The sirens wailed their warning. The bombs fell indiscriminately on offices, shops and houses. For four months Britons saw their cities on fire, fine churches burnt to a shell, great buildings collapsed into the street, private homes turned into a chaos of crushed bricks, charred wood, and broken glass. But despite the long, severe and often frightening raids, British morale was not broken.

Hitler's belief that he could persuade the British to beg for peace was an illusion. The terror of the bombing served only to strengthen the determination of the people. Churchill epitomized this determination in a broadcast which he made at the height of the London blitz: 'These cruel, wanton, indiscriminate bombings of London are, of course, a part of Hitler's invasion plans. He hopes, by killing large numbers of civilians, and women and children, that he will terrorize and cow the people of this mighty imperial city, and make them a burden and an anxiety to the Government and thus distract our attention unduly from the ferocious onslaught he is preparing. Little does he know the spirit of the British nation, or the tough fibre of the Londoners, whose forebears played a leading part in the establishment of Parliamentary institutions and who have been bred to value freedom far above their lives. This wicked man, the repository and embodiment of many forms of soul-destroying hatred, this monstrous product of former wrongs and shame, has now resolved to try to break our famous island race by a process of indiscriminate slaughter and destruction. What he has done is to kindle a fire in British hearts, here and all over the world, which will glow long after all traces of the conflagration he has caused in London have been removed. He has lighted a fire which will burn with a steady and consuming flame until the last vestiges of Nazi tyranny have been burnt out of Europe, and until the Old World—and the New—can join hands to rebuild the temples of man's freedom and man's honour, upon foundations which will not soon or easily be overthrown.'

The British blitz was the most sustained onslaught that Hitler had yet delivered on any country during over a year of war. By the end of the year over twenty thousand people had been killed. But the blitz had failed. The British did not intend to surrender. Of course they hated being bombed and bludgeoned.

But the thought of Nazi rule appealed to them even less. Despite their hardships, they began to make fun of the Nazis and their leader. They learned to scorn Hitler's threats, and drew derisive cartoons of him and his fellow Nazis. At the height of their misfortunes, the British people found comfort in jokes and laughter.

6

Italy Strikes

MUSSOLINI had watched closely from the first day of the invasion of Poland. He envied Hitler's swift military success. Although he had originally promised Germany full support, he nevertheless stood aside, remaining neutral. He was reluctant to give his 'ally' any significant help. When Hitler invaded France, Mussolini again did nothing. Again he watched and waited. It was only when France was on the verge of surrender that he ordered his army to attack. This Italian 'stab in the back' was a callous move which shocked the western world.

Mussolini sought what he hoped would be a more 'glorious' victory: one which Italy could win on its own. He did not want merely to pick at the bones of Hitler's victims. He was eager to show the world that he could be as successful a conqueror as Hitler. He therefore decided to invade Greece. In this way he hoped to advance towards his goal of an Italian-controlled Mediterranean. He would copy the emperors of ancient Rome, and turn the Mediterranean into an 'Italian Lake'.

At the height of the London blitz the newspapers reported that Mussolini had attacked Greece. This event seemed remote to those who were being bombed night by night with increasing severity. But the Italian attack on Greece was important for Britain. In 1939 the British Government had promised to defend the Greeks against invasion. In the past Britain had been a friend of Greece. It was with British help that the Greeks won their independence from the Turks a hundred years before. Now, at the very moment when Britain itself was in grave danger, Greece too was threatened with violence and conquest.

March 1940: Hitler and Mussolini meet to discuss the war. Mussolini resented
Hitler's easy victories; Hitler despised his fellow-dictator.

The Greeks were not afraid of Mussolini. They knew that the
Italians were not as military-minded as the Germans. They saw
that Italian Fascism was not as savage as German Nazism.
Courageously, and successfully, they faced up to the invading
army. The Italians were soon halted. To the surprise of the on-
looking world, the Greeks then advanced. They drove the Italian
troops out of Greece and back into their own territory, Albania.
The Greeks were elated by success. So were the conquered nations
of Europe. At last a dictator state had been shown that military

aggression did not always succeed. Nor were the Greeks content to drive out the Italian armies. They went further, invading and conquering a large part of Italian Albania.

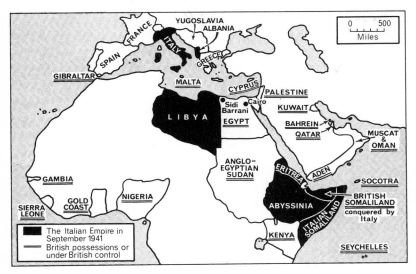

The Italian Empire, December 1940

The Greek defeat of the Italians was a tonic for those in Britain. Mussolini had not been idle in Africa, where his Empire included Abyssinia, Italian Somaliland and Libya. He looked with greed across his African borders on to British territory. In August Mussolini ordered the Italians to sieze British Somaliland. The British forces were too small to resist, and the Italian troops soon won an easy victory. They also advanced over the borders of Kenya and the Sudan. A month later, elated by this success, Mussolini ordered his troops to drive the British out of Egypt. There were 250,000 Italian soldiers in Libya. They outnumbered the British forces in Egypt. Optimistically, Mussolini's army advanced across the desert. Throughout November the outlook for Britain was as bleak in Africa as it was at home. The Italians crossed into Egypt, and advanced towards the Suez Canal.

On 8 December 1940 it seemed that Mussolini might ride in triumph through the streets of Cairo before the end of the year; that he might, like Napoleon, stand in the shadow of the pyramids as their conqueror. Three days later the Italian dream was over.

1942: Australians advance across the desert, helping to drive the Italians out of Egypt, and capturing half of Mussolini's 250,000 men.

Just as the Greeks had stood up to an Italian attack two months before, so now the British did likewise. At the desert town of Sidi Barrani they halted the Italian advance. The Italians were then driven back across the desert, leaving three generals and 6,000 soldiers behind as prisoners-of-war. The Royal Navy shelled the Italians as they retreated back along the coast towards Libya. The Royal Air Force struck at their supply depots inland. 20,000 more Italians were taken prisoner before their retreat from Egypt was complete.

The year 1940 thus came to an end with both a Greek and a British victory over Mussolini. These successes were cause for satisfaction. But Hitler was still unbeaten. True, the Germans had not yet invaded Britain, despite their threats and boasting. They had failed to destroy the air power of the Royal Air Force. They had also failed to break British morale by three months of terror bombing. But in Europe, their armies stood as yet undefeated. They were, indeed, refreshed by their many victories. They were ready to march, ready to conquer yet more territory if Hitler should so desire.

In occupied Europe the cruel Nazi regime continued to perse-cute all those it controlled. The peoples of Poland, Czechoslovakia, Denmark, Norway, Holland, Belgium, Luxembourg and France lived under the savage shadow of the Swastika. Russia continued to send Germany vast quantities of petrol, grain and timber in return for peace. Even the unconquered countries, Rumania, Hungary, Yugoslavia and Bulgaria, came more and more under German control. In only fifteen months of war, Hitler had achieved the virtual mastery of Europe.

7

The United States and the War

DURING the first fifteen months of the war in Europe the United States remained neutral. It did not intend to become militarily involved in a far-off European quarrel. Despite President Roosevelt's strong belief in democracy, and his deep hatred of tyranny, many of the people whom he led had no wish to fight against Hitler. They would not cast their votes for war.

American isolationist feeling was too strong for Roosevelt to ignore. Many sensible Americans felt that since 1918 the nations of Europe had wasted too many opportunities. They had failed to become good neighbours among themselves. Other Americans, equally sincere, were hostile towards the British and French Empires. They saw them as a form of dictatorship which restricted the liberties of Indians or Burmese or Africans in the same way that Hitler restricted Jewish liberties. They saw no reason why American soldiers should risk their lives to preserve the French or British Empires. The American Ambassador to Britain, Joseph Kennedy, held this view strongly. In writing to Roosevelt he poured doubt on Britain's power to resist. He gave the impression that Britain was a broken reed.

Shortly after Hitler invaded Poland, Roosevelt told the United States Congress: 'Our acts must be guided by one single hard-headed thought—keeping America out of this war.' When, in June 1940, the German armies reached the outskirts of Paris, Roosevelt rejected strong French and British appeals for immediate aid. His decision reflected the wishes of the American people.

But with the London blitz there came a change. American opinion
was stirred by the vivid newspaper and film reports of London
under attack, of Britain standing alone against Germany, of an
island clearly preparing by itself to meet the invasion.

British pluck and endurance won wide American admiration.
Even staunch isolationists were shocked by pictures of the City
of London in flames and of St. Paul's cathedral framed in smoke
and fire. They were shaken too by the frequent news of German
submarine sinkings in the Atlantic. Many Americans now asked:
'Might not the United States be next on the German list?' Of
course they were citizens of a large country, rich, powerful and
remote from Europe. But they had only to look at a map to see
how much territory Germany already controlled. They were still
unwilling to join the war directly. They still refused to send troops
to die or ships to be torpedoed. But at the same time they became
more and more prepared, and even eager, to help Britain in
distress.

In September 1940, at the beginning of the blitz, Britain and the
United States came to a small but significant agreement. Churchill
gave Roosevelt a number of pieces of British land on which to
set up American naval and air bases. Britain gave these bases free
of charge. America could keep them for ninety-nine years, until
the year 2039. The land was part of the many British possessions
near the American continent. These new bases enabled the United
States to extend its own defensive network considerably. As a
result, Americans became more secure against a German attack.
In return for these bases the United States gave Britain fifty
destroyers. These ships were old ones. Most of them were in a bad
state of repair. But they were desperately needed. The British
were glad that the United States, though still not a military ally,
was at last giving material support. For their part, the Americans
had at last made it clear that they did not wish to see Britain
collapse.

Roosevelt decided to give Britain all the help possible, short
of the United States itself going to war. In a speech to the American
people in December 1940 he put the issues bluntly and convinc-
ingly. 'If Great Britain goes down,' said Roosevelt, 'the Axis
powers will control the continents of Europe, Asia, Africa,
Australasia, and the high seas—and they will be in a position to
bring enormous military and naval resources against this hemi-
sphere. It is no exaggeration to say that all of us, in all the

Americas, would be living at the point of a gun—a gun loaded with explosive bullets, economic as well as military. . . . Frankly and definitely there is danger ahead—danger against which we must prepare. But we well know that we cannot escape danger, or the fear of danger, by crawling into bed and pulling the covers over our heads. . . . The people of Europe who are defending themselves do not ask us to do their fighting. They ask us for the implements of war, the planes, the tanks, the guns, the freighters which will enable them to fight for their liberty and for our security. Emphatically we must get these weapons to them in sufficient volume and quickly enough, so that we and our children will be saved the agony and suffering of war which others have had to endure.'

The hub of American aid to Britain was the Lend-Lease Act. This became law on 11 March 1941. Under Lend-Lease, Britain could 'loan' vital war materials for as long as the war might last. Through Lend-Lease, Britain was soon able to replenish her dwindling stocks of food, machine tools and even tobacco. At first the imports under Lend-Lease were small. But by the end of the war the United States had provided Britain with half its tanks, most of its transport aircraft, a quarter of its ammunition and almost all its extra shipping. This was a vital contribution to Britain's war effort. Churchill called Lend-Lease 'the most unsordid act in the history of any nation'.

While Britain stood alone in the democratic cause, two Americans, father and son, surveyed the British scene. The father, Joseph Kennedy, had just completed four years as Roosevelt's Ambassador to Britain. The son, John F. Kennedy, had just written a book on contemporary Britain. Ambassador Kennedy broadcast to the American people in January 1941. He told them that in his experienced view there were 'serious obstacles' in the way of a British victory. He wanted the United States to stand clear. 'I oppose the entry of this country into the present war,' he said. 'England is not fighting our battle. This is not our war. We were not consulted when it began. We have no veto power over its continuance.'

The Ambassador doubted whether the United States could ever send enough men to Europe to make up the balance between Germany's strength and Britain's weakness. He contrasted the 6,000,000 Germans under arms with only 1,500,000 Britons. For him the moral was, 'Stay out of war'. But his son, the future

President, was not so pessimistic. Although he was then only twenty-three years old, he knew the mettle of the British people better than his father did. He lacked his father's experience. But he did not lack wisdom of his own.

In his book, published after the fall of France, the young John F. Kennedy stressed the awakening which took place in Britain as soon as Churchill became Prime Minister: 'All the latent energy stored up in England during the last seven years is being expanded in a vigorous drive for victory. Industry and labour, the rich and the poor, are contributing to England's fight for survival, with the knowledge that this is the supreme test of democracy's ability to survive in this changing world.' The old Kennedy wished to wash his hands of Europe. The young Kennedy saw more clearly that America too was threatened by Hitler's victories, and must play a vital part in defending democracy.

8

The Growing Storm

STRENGTHENED by the knowledge that American help was on its way, the British decided to drive the Italians out of East Africa altogether. They hoped to re-conquer British Somaliland, and the border towns of Kenya and the Sudan which the Italians had occupied in the autumn of 1940. They also hoped to liberate Abyssinia itself from Italian rule. Much sympathy had been aroused amongst the democracies for the Abyssinian people, after the Italians had invaded their country in 1935. The Italian conquest of Abyssinia was the first aggressive act of the period leading up to the Second World War. The re-conquest of Abyssinia would therefore have symbolic as well as strategic importance. It would show the dictators, that in the end, and sooner than they had imagined, the fruits of their aggression would be taken from them. It would also enable the British to build up another supply base, far from German hands, which would help secure the protection of Egypt from any future German attack.

The Italians held many strongly fortified positions in Abyssinia. But slowly they were driven from them. British troops were not alone. They were joined by Africans from the Gold Coast (now Ghana), Nigeria and Rhodesia, and by Belgian soldiers who had escaped from Hitler's clutches. The South African Air Force joined the Royal Air Force in reconnaissance work. They searched for Italian fortified positions in the rough, wild countryside. In less than five months the Italians were driven out of the country which they had conquered only six years before. The Red Sea was now entirely under British control. The supply route from Britain to India was more secure. Mussolini had suffered his third defeat of the war.

But it was not enough to defeat the Italians. Germany was the real enemy of the democracies. Germany was the power which tyrannized Europe. It was Germany which, by the end of July 1941, had sunk over seven million tons of British, and even neutral, shipping, making the Atlantic an ocean of fear and danger. It was German pilots who still bombed British cities and killed British civilians. It was German action which had brought the United States into such close association with Britain. American ships now escorted British vessels on their 3,000 mile journey across the Atlantic from Iceland to the United States. American sailors shared the perils which German submarines brought to that long and lonely journey.

In April 1941 Roosevelt took Greenland under American protection, to prevent the Germans building bases there. Three months later he occupied Iceland, which Britain had already controlled for nearly a year. The more ships Hitler sank, the more British towns he bombed, the closer he drew Britain and the United States to each other. There were twice as many Americans as Germans. This meant twice as many factory workers, twice as many sailors, twice as many pilots. And while the German people faced the dangers of increased British bombing, not a single German bomb ever fell on the United States. Its factories could work all-out for war without fear of bombs and fire.

Hitler's control of Europe was almost complete. Its raw materials poured into his factories. Rumanian oil, French coal, the agricultural produce of Belgium, Holland and Bulgaria, forced labour from Poland, Slovakia and indeed most of Europe, as well as the constant flow of supplies from Russia, all increased German power and confidence. But Hitler was angry that he had failed to conquer

Britain, and angry too that Mussolini was so incompetent a dictator in the military sphere. As a result of the Italian defeats, Britain now controlled the eastern Mediterranean. Greece, Crete, Cyprus, Palestine, Egypt and much of Libya were under either British or Greek control. Hitler therefore decided that he would finish the job at which the Italians had proved so incompetent. In March 1941 he forced the British out of Libya, driving them back to the Egyptian border. Next, he decided to conquer Greece, where Mussolini's armies had been put to shame five months before.

There was little doubt that Hitler would be able, with his superior military power, to destroy Greek independence. But his troops had to get there, and their route lay through Yugoslavia. Since 1939 the Yugoslav Government had accepted all Germany's demands. It sent its agricultural produce to Germany in the quantities which Germany demanded. It did nothing to resist German economic control. The borders of Yugoslavia provided no security. Bulgaria, Rumania and Hungary had thrown in their lot with Germany. In the north there was a common border with Germany itself. To both the south and west Italy waited with grasping hands, hoping to take over parts of Yugoslavia for herself, and to make the Adriatic yet another Italian lake. Italian troops were poised in Albania, and at Zara, ready to strike. Surrounded by enemies, the Yugoslavs accepted a pro-German policy as a necessity, however unpleasant.

The Yugoslavs are a proud people. After three hundred years of Turkish rule they had won their independence in the nineteenth century. Their country was not rich in natural resources. Some of its provinces were remote, poor and backward. But they prized their independence. They were ashamed of making common cause with the Germans.

In March 1941 two Yugoslav ministers travelled to Vienna and signed an agreement with Germany. They promised to put their economy entirely under German control. They agreed to allow German troops to use Yugoslav railways for their attack on Greece. The Yugoslav people were humiliated by what their Government had done. Not only did the agreement mean that Yugoslavia would fall even more tightly under German control, but also that it would play its part in helping Germany to destroy Greek independence. The Greeks too had won their independence from the Turks after a long struggle. The Greeks were also a Balkan

Map labels: GERMANY, SWITZ., HUNGARY, Zagreb, CROATIA, Belgrade, RUMANIA, Zara, YUGOSLAVIA, ITALY, Adriatic Sea, BULGARIA, ALBANIA, Skopje, Salonika, GREECE, TURKEY, Aegean Sea, Ionian Sea, Athens, DODECANESE ISLANDS (Italian), Cape Matapan, CRETE

0 — 150 Miles

Countries attacking Yugoslavia and Greece

Yugoslavia and Greece, 1941

people, living in an equally poor land, struggling with equal courage to maintain themselves as an independent people.

Overnight Yugoslavia rebelled. The pro-German Government was overthrown. The people demanded a policy of resistance to Germany. They appealed to Britain for help. They knew their resistance would be short-lived. They realized Hitler would crush them with little difficulty. They knew that Greece too must succumb sooner or later to German attack.

The Yugoslavs knew that many of them would die. But a British author, Rebecca West, who knew them well, understood why they were prepared to face death: 'This was not the ultimate consideration. For some day the rule of Hitler must pass; it would not endure for ever. Then, if Yugoslavia had moved against Hitler with pride and courage, those that conquered him would have to admit it as a comrade and grant it the right to exist in whatever new order of Europe might be instituted. But if Yugoslavs behaved like cowards, no one would respect them, not even themselves, and they would remain abased for ever. . . . They chose that Yugoslavia should be destroyed rather than submit to Germany and be secure, and they made that choice for love of life and not love of death. . . . The news that Hitler had been defied by Yugoslavia travelled like sunshine over the countries which he had devoured and humiliated, promising spring.'

On 6 April 1941, at dawn, German bombers attacked the Yugoslav capital, Belgrade. In only three days of bombing over 20,000 Yugoslav civilians were killed. German troops advanced rapidly, looting and burning as they went. Their greedy 'allies', Hungary, Bulgaria and Italy attacked Yugoslavia at the same time. In the Yugoslav province of Croatia another 'quisling', Ante Pavelic, agreed to establish a pro-Nazi government. He welcomed the Germans to the Croat capital, Zagreb, with flowers. Meanwhile, German planes methodically destroyed the hospitals, the university, the churches and the schools of Belgrade. After twelve days Yugoslavia surrendered. Germany had claimed another victim. Tyranny had advanced to another frontier. Courage and independence had received another setback.

The German armies did not pause on their march southwards. Fresh from their victory over Yugoslavia, they pressed on into Greece. Again they were joined by greedy neighbours, Bulgaria and Italy, each anxious to take advantage of German strength. The British hastened to fulfil their obligations to Greece. A small British force tried to hold the German advance near Salonika, but in vain. The British and Greek troops were driven back southwards to the sea. The British tried to hold the Greek island of Crete as a defensive position in the eastern Mediterranean. But after eleven days of fierce fighting that too fell into German hands. In six weeks Germany had conquered two more independent states. The Balkans were unable to resist any longer than western Europe had resisted a year before. As Berlin radio announced in triumph, 'the Swastika flies over the Acropolis.'

Hitler's victory cast a gloomy shadow over his enemies. But all was not lost for the democratic cause. Britain still controlled Cyprus, Palestine, Egypt and Malta. Despite the rapid German success in the Balkans, Hitler's mastery did not extend beyond Europe. British ships were still able to move from one end of the Mediterranean to the other. In the Atlantic, all the skill and daring of German submarine commanders could not stop the steady flow of food and war supplies to Britain. The rapidly growing number of British planes, and the improved British air defences, ensured that German bombers were seen less and less above the cities of Britain. German rule brought terror from the North

Cape to Cape Matapan, from the mouth of the Loire to the mouth of the Vistula. But despite his parade of victories, Hitler was a prisoner in the very Europe which he controlled.

9

Russia under Attack

WHAT did Hitler wish to achieve in Europe? Were there any limits to his ambition? Did he really expect to become master of the whole world? There is no clear answer to these questions. Hitler's mind worked along obscure lines. As a result, German policy was often muddled and contradictory.

Hitler began his political career with relatively limited aims. He wanted to restore German prestige after the defeat of 1918, and also to make Germany the most powerful nation in Europe. This he had done. He wanted to drive the Jews out of German life. This he had achieved. He wanted to show the world that Germans recognized no outside control, no foreign tutelage, no international restrictions on their actions. He had made this abundantly clear. By May 1941 all Europe feared Hitler, and acted as Germany commanded. Britain did not have the power to invade. The United States was unlikely to declare war. The German people acclaimed Hitler as the architect of their new greatness. The Jews, who had been expelled to special areas in Poland, were beaten, humiliated, herded like cattle into concentration camps, and shot dead at German whim. What more could Hitler want?

To the east of Germany lay Russia, silent and afraid. The Russian people wanted to be left in peace. More than twenty years of rigid Communist rule had exhausted them. Their leader, Stalin, had made it a crime for them to have independent thoughts. Cruel purges had eliminated thousands of the more imaginative, more critical Russians. Writers, factory managers, army officers, university teachers, priests, had all been shot or imprisoned if they dared to speak out against Stalin's tyranny.

Hitler looked at Russia with greedy eyes. The well-being of the

Russian people meant nothing to him. He regarded them as inferior, sub-human, expendable—like the Jews. But he was eager to possess the wide grain lands of the Ukraine, the oil fields of the Caucasus, the coalfields of the Don Bas, the steel centres of the Dnieper valley and the shipbuilding yards of the Black Sea coast. Along the Volga and in the Urals the Russians had developed great industrial centres, chemical plants, truck and tractor factories, textile mills and coalfields. In the sphere of food, Russia produced over a quarter of the world's wheat, rye, oats and potatoes.

Hitler wanted to conquer Russian industry in order to strengthen the German economy. He wanted Russian food to fill German stomachs. He wanted Russian farms to belong to German farmers and Russian cities to bustle with German settlers. He knew that it would be difficult, perhaps impossible, to conquer the British Empire. But he still intended to create an empire of his own. He would be the founder of the German empire in Asia. And after his death it would survive for a thousand years.

The Russians were in no way prepared for a German attack. Stalin believed that Hitler would honour his promise not to invade Russia. He hoped that Hitler would exhaust himself in a long, inconclusive, wasteful war with Britain. The purges had weakened the higher command of the Russian army and lowered Russian morale. Strong anti-Communist feeling in the Ukraine made it almost certain that many Russians would welcome Hitler as their liberator, and even help him against the Soviet regime.

Stalin refused to listen to the warnings which came from Britain and elsewhere, of German plans to invade Russia in the summer of 1941. He refused to believe that Hitler would risk the fate of Napoleon by sending his armies into the vast Russian spaces, where the snow and ice of winter were as dangerous for an invader as the opposition of the most able general or the most powerful army.

Hitler believed that once he had destroyed Russia, his position in the world would be indestructible. The German Empire would then link up with the Japanese in Asia and threaten the British in India. By conquering Russia, Hitler believed, Germany would soon become as powerful, if not more so, than the United States. It would produce more planes and tanks than any other nation in the world. Its ability to invade Britain would be revived. Its chances of conquering Britain would be enhanced. 'If *we* want to rule,' Hitler told a friend as early as 1934, 'we must first conquer Russia.' Now he felt able to do so. 'You have only to kick in the door,' he told one of his generals in 1941, 'and the whole rotten structure will come crashing down.'

At dawn on 22 June 1941 the Germans launched their invasion of Russia. Hungarians, Rumanians, Italians and later Finns joined in the attack. The Russians, caught unprepared, reeled backwards. Of Russia's 6,000 planes, 2,000 were destroyed on the ground within two days. It looked as if Hitler's dream would soon and easily be fulfilled. Eight days later, on Hitler's birthday, the Russian defences were finally broken. The Germans were elated by this rapid success. Hitler told his generals that as a result of the German victory over Russia Churchill was likely to be overthrown in Britain. He was convinced that a new British Government would be called into office to make peace with the triumphant Germany.

By October 1941 a German victory seemed certain. 'The enemy in the east,' Hitler confidently announced, 'has been struck down and will never rise again. Behind our troops there already lies a territory twice the size of Germany when I came to power in 1933.' His boast was accurate. The German armies were on the outskirts of Leningrad and Moscow. The rich Ukraine had been brought under German control. A million Russians had been killed or taken prisoner. Over two million had deserted to the Germans.

But Hitler was too confident of absolute victory. He failed to take advantage of the strong anti-Communist feeling in the Ukraine. He failed to give the anti-Communist Russians an 'independent' state which would have made them his friends and allies. Instead, most captured Russians were treated with great cruelty, beaten, put to forced labour, starved and murdered in vast numbers. Hitler went so far as to say that 'anyone who talks about cherishing the local inhabitant and civilizing him goes straight off into a concentration camp'. Hitler believed that Germany had no need to offer the Russians either mercy or compromise. Like the Poles, like the Jews, like all against whom he had nourished a hatred, the Russians must die. 'This sounds cruel,' Hitler explained to a Nazi official, 'but such is the law of life.'

Hitler's view of the 'law of life' was understood by his subordinates. In the occupied areas of Russia the Germans behaved with the utmost cruelty. Their atrocities horrified, and unified, the Russian people. With every prisoner-of-war whom the Germans shot while in captivity, with every woman or child they killed as a reprisal, with every farm they burnt to the ground, the Russian determination to resist was strengthened. Hitler's terror made Russia forget Stalin's severity. Faced with German cruelty on an unprecedented scale, the spirit of the Russian people, which had fallen so low under Communist rule, revived and grew. Once again the old medieval rhyme was heard across the vast territory of Russia:

> 'Russian! Russian! Wake up! Wake up!
> The German comes. The uninvited guest.'

10

Russia at War

By October 1941 Hitler was confident that he would defeat Russia. He forecast victory, if not that winter, then certainly by the end of 1942. But his confidence was misplaced.

Russia was not alone in its struggle. It was true that many people in Britain thought it best to let Germany and Russia fight it out to the finish; to so exhaust each other in battle that both Nazism and Communism would crumble. But Churchill thought otherwise. He knew the added danger to Britain if Hitler were victorious in Russia. For Britain would then be next on the list.

Churchill was convinced that the Russian people would be made stronger by adversity. He had seen the flagging British spirit revive under the worst of the German air-raids in 1940. He was convinced that the greater the German terror, the more ferocious would be the Russian resistance. He therefore decided against standing aside. As he saw it, Britain's interest lay in giving Russia all the help possible. In one of his most important war speeches he told the British people, and the world:

'No one has been a more consistent opponent of Communism

than I have for the last twenty-five years. I will unsay no word that I have spoken about it. But all this fades away before the spectacle which is now unfolding. The past with its crimes, its follies and its tragedies, flashes away. I see the Russian soldiers standing on the threshold of their native land, guarding the fields which their fathers have tilled from time immemorial. I see them guarding their homes where mothers and wives pray—ah yes, for there are times when all pray—for the safety of their loved ones, the return of the breadwinner, of their champion, of their protector. I see the ten thousand villages of Russia, where the means of existence was wrung so hardly from the soil, but where there are still primordial human joys, where maidens laugh and children play. I see advancing upon all this in hideous onslaught the Nazi war machine, with its clanking, heel-clicking, dandified Prussian officers, its crafty expert agents fresh from the cowing and tying-down of a dozen countries. I see also the dull, drilled, docile, brutish masses of the Hun soldiery plodding on like a swarm of crawling locusts. . . .

'Now I have to declare the decision of His Majesty's Government. . . . I have to make the declaration, but can you doubt what our policy will be? We have but one aim and one single, irrevocable purpose. We are resolved to destroy Hitler and every vestige of the Nazi regime. From this nothing will turn us— nothing. We will never parley, we will never negotiate with Hitler or any of his gang. We shall fight him by land, we shall fight him by sea, we shall fight him in the air, until with God's help we have rid the earth of his shadow and liberated its peoples from his yoke. Any man or state who fights on against Nazidom will have our aid. Any man or state who marches with Hitler is our foe. . . . That is our policy and that is our declaration. It follows, therefore, that we shall give whatever help we can to Russia and the Russian people. We shall appeal to all our friends and allies in every part of the world to take the same course and pursue it, as we shall, faithfully and steadfastly to the end.'

The British applauded Churchill's decision. They welcomed Russia as an ally. For over a year they had fought alone against Hitler. Now the Russians were with them. Russia's resistance quickly won their admiration. Despite their own hardships, the British Government immediately offered Russia all the military and economic help which they could spare. Within a year they were able to send Russia over 2,400 tanks and 1,800 planes.

To relieve the pressure of the German assault on Russia, Churchill promised Stalin that Britain would 'bomb Germany by day as well as by night in ever-increasing measure, casting upon them month by month a heavier discharge of bombs, and making the German people taste and gulp each month a sharper dose of the miseries which they have showered on mankind'. All this was done, and more. Although the United States was still neutral, it was persuaded to send important supplies to Russia, including 2,000 tanks, 1,300 planes and a wide range of essential supplies from thousands of lorries to millions of boots.

Both Russia and Britain were strengthened by having an ally in the other, and a partner in the United States. For all his boasting and self-confidence, Hitler was surely no match for these three powers combined? Despite the busy, murderous work of German torpedoes, British ships still reached Russia through the Arctic ports, the Persian Gulf and the Far East. Despite the rapid advance of the German armies, Leningrad, Moscow and Stalingrad were never captured. Equally important, no German soldier ever set foot in the great industrial complex in the Urals or in the growing cities of Siberia. Of the Volga cities only Stalingrad was reduced to rubble. But Saratov, Kuibyshev, Kazan, Gorki and the other manufacturing centres remained under Russian control, their war industries busy. The oilfields of Baku stayed in Russian hands throughout the war, feeding the Russian armies with vital fuel. Allied supplies flowed into Russia uninterruptedly across the thousands of miles of open frontiers which Hitler could not touch.

The Russians made full use of outside aid. But they saved Russia by their own exertions. In November 1941 fresh, well-trained troops were hurried forward from Siberia for the successful defence of Moscow. Leningrad survived three years of siege and terrible suffering, losing almost a million of its inhabitants from starvation or bombardment. A German army of 330,000 men was defeated in the streets of Stalingrad, and Hitler's plan to advance up the Volga had to be abandoned.

In the woods and marshes of the Ukraine and White Russia another barrier to German victory sprang up. By 1943 over half a million Russian partisans were fighting tenaciously in German-held territory against the German occupation forces. They risked torture and cruel death. But they succeeded in dislocating the whole German supply system. In only four months in 1943 they

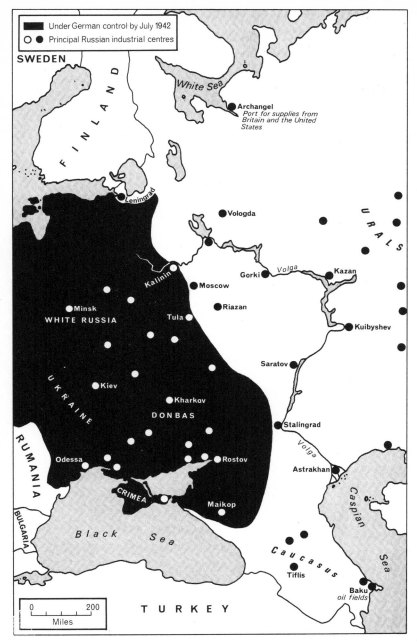

Under German control by July 1942
O ● Principal Russian industrial centres

SWEDEN

FINLAND

White Sea

Archangel
*Port for supplies from
Britain and the United
States*

Leningrad

●Vologda

U R A L S

Kalinin

Gorki   *Volga*   ●Kazan

●Moscow

●Minsk

WHITE RUSSIA   Tula

●Riazan

●Kuibyshev

UKRAINE

●Kiev

Saratov

●Kharkov

DONBAS

Stalingrad

Volga

Odessa

●Rostov

Astrakhan

RUMANIA

CRIMEA

Maikop

Caspian

BULGARIA

Black   Sea

C a u c a s u s

Sea

Tiflis

Baku
oil fields

0   200

Miles

T U R K E Y

The Germans in Russia, 1942

1943: a German officer and his men pause during anti-partisan operations in Russia. Over a million partisans were killed while fighting behind the German lines.

destroyed or damaged 72 railway bridges, wrecked 814 railway engines and derailed over 1,000 trains. The courage and skill of these partisans demoralized the Germans, who slowly withdrew from large areas nominally within their control. Even the much-persecuted Jews formed partisan groups of their own, and struck at the Germans where they could.

The Germans murdered thousands of Russian women and children in an attempt to destroy the partisans' will to fight. But the partisan war went on. Leningrad survived. Stalingrad was never captured. The impetus of the German attack was broken. Russian courage was restored. The long, slow march to victory had begun.

In 1943 Hitler was asked by one of his generals, 'My Führer, why do you want to attack in the east at all this year?' 'You are quite right,' Hitler replied. 'Whenever I think of this attack my stomach turns over.' Hitler had learnt a savage lesson. Russia could not be conquered as easily as he imagined.

In 1812 Napoleon complained that it was the Russian winter which defeated him. Hitler hoped to spare his troops the need for fighting in the severe cold. He expected them to be able to spend the winter, as victors, in the warm cities of Leningrad and

Russian children plant cabbages in the centre of Leningrad. During the three years in which the Germans besieged the city over 800,000 civilians were starved to death or were killed by shells and bombs.

Moscow. But the Russians did not fall back as he forecast. The war in the east went on all winter. The Russians were used to the cold. They were properly equipped to fight in snow blizzards.

November 1941: Russian troops, prepared both for the advance of winter and arrival of the Germans, man a machine-gun mounted on a sledge. They are wearing white cloaks as camouflage.

They knew how to live in a world of frozen rivers and icy winds.

At the end of October 1941 the German army admitted that 'weather conditions have entailed a temporary halt in the advance'. A German doctor at the front line wrote enviously of 'the Russian who is completely at home . . . in the wilds. Give him an axe and a knife and in a few hours he will do anything, run up a sledge, a stretcher, a little igloo . . . make a stove out of a couple of old oil cans. Our men just stand about miserably burning the precious petrol to keep warm. At night they gather in the few wooden houses which are still standing. Several times we found the sentries had fallen asleep . . . literally frozen to death.' The German generals could not provide adequate shelter, clothing or food for their men.

In the summer of 1941 Hitler was confident that the Germans could destroy Russia. Not all his officers felt as he did, even then. One, a colonel, wrote pessimistically: 'The German army in fighting Russia is like an elephant attacking a host of ants. The elephant will kill thousands, perhaps even millions of ants, but in the end their numbers will overcome him, and he will be eaten to the bone.'

Hitler was at the height of his powers when he launched his attack upon Russia. But by his attack, he threw away all chance of world dominion. He could not defeat the combination of Russian bravery, allied supplies, partisan activity and the fierce winter. Hitler's invasion of Russia was proof of his success, his daring, his ambition and his confidence. It was also his first, and worst, mistake. By invading Russia, he lost the war.

11

Japan

AFTER 1840 the Far East was the scene of widespread imperial conquest. By 1900 the French ruled in Indo-China, the Dutch in Indonesia, the Americans in the Philippines, the British in India, Burma, Malaya and Borneo, the Australians in New Guinea. China had been forced to give special trading rights to foreigners in forty or fifty of its largest towns. Only one oriental people had never been conquered or interfered with: the Japanese.

Japan's independence was a source of admiration for the people of Asia. Its industrial growth showed that Asians could become as efficient, as prosperous and as powerful as any European. The great powers of Europe accepted Japan as an equal. Its ambassadors represented Japanese interests all over the world. Britain even welcomed Japan as an ally in 1902. Millions of Asians living under foreign domination hoped to emulate Japan's achievements. Japan was a visible example to the subject people of Asia of what they might do once the 'foreign devils' were removed.

But Japan's success did not come from trade and treaties alone. Much of its power sprang from conquest. In 1895 it had seized Formosa from China. In 1905 it defeated the Russians and established Japanese influence over Manchuria. In 1910 it annexed Korea. After the First World War the victors gave it control over most of Germany's islands in the Pacific Ocean, in particular the Marianas. These gains stimulated Japanese ambition. Many Japanese wanted even more land. They wanted to expand their industry and settle their rapidly growing population on the Asian mainland. They wanted to control the rich mineral wealth of the Far East. Some Japanese argued in favour of expansion at the expense of China. Others felt that it would be easier and more profitable to expand southwards into the territory ruled by Holland, Britain, France and the United States.

After the First World War the Japanese felt humiliated by Britain's refusal to renew the Anglo-Japanese alliance. They also resented the growing discrimination in the United States against oriental immigrants. They felt the need to show the rest of the world that the 'yellow' man was as worthy of respect and admiration as the 'white'. But their method of winning this respect included the invasion of their 'yellow' neighbour, China, in 1937. For four years their armies advanced through China. Like the Germans, they used terror bombing of civilians to help their conquests. But despite great territorial losses, the Chinese refused to surrender.

Although Britain and the United States were not prepared to take military action against Japan in 1937, they greatly admired the bravery of China's apparently hopeless resistance. By 1940 they were sending China substantial military aid. This did not stop Japan annexing large areas of China, rich in coal, iron and

A Chinese soldier examines a comrade killed during a Japanese attack. Over two million Chinese were killed during the eight years of war with Japan.

chemicals. But it did link the fate of China with that of the western democracies.

After four years of cruel war, the Japanese were still not masters of China. They therefore began to look elsewhere for an easier area of expansion. South-east Asia was rich in the minerals and food which Japan lacked. Ninety per cent of the world's rubber and 60 per cent of the world's tin came from the Dutch East Indies and British Malaya. The widespread Asian territory ruled by American and the European imperial powers produced oil, coal, iron, timber, rice and tea. To conquer these valuable territories Japan would need to defeat Britain and the United States. Surely this was not an easy task to undertake, with large numbers of troops already tied down in China, and thousands of miles of ocean to cross and to control? But the difficulties were overlooked in the excitement of further conquests.

In July 1941 the Japanese took their first step towards a wider war in Asia. For over a year French Indo-China (now Vietnam,

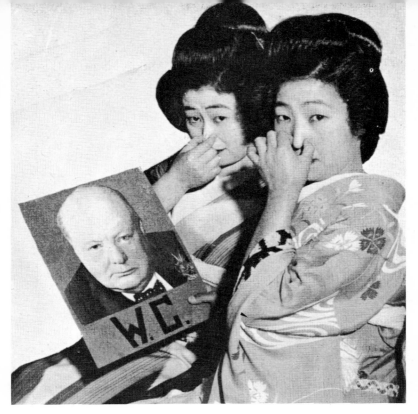

January 1941: Britain and Japan are not yet at war, but in Tokyo two Japanese girls give their opinion of the British Prime Minister. This photograph was published by the Japanese as official propaganda.

Laos and Cambodia) had been ruled by the pro-German Vichy authorities. The Japanese, allied with Germany, forced the Vichy administration to accept a Japanese occupation of Saigon. A glance at the map reveals the danger which this move represented to the British, Dutch and United States possessions in south-east Asia.

In retaliation against the Japanese occupation of Indo-China the Americans closed the Panama Canal to Japanese ships. Britain, Holland and the United States refused to let Japan buy the oil, rubber and tin which it would need to conduct a major war. The Japanese Government were divided as to their future policy. The Prime Minister wanted to negotiate a settlement with the United States, even if this meant ending the war against China. The War Minister wanted to launch an attack on south-east Asia immediately. The Emperor Hirohito listened to both views. He feared that the army would seize power if he opted for

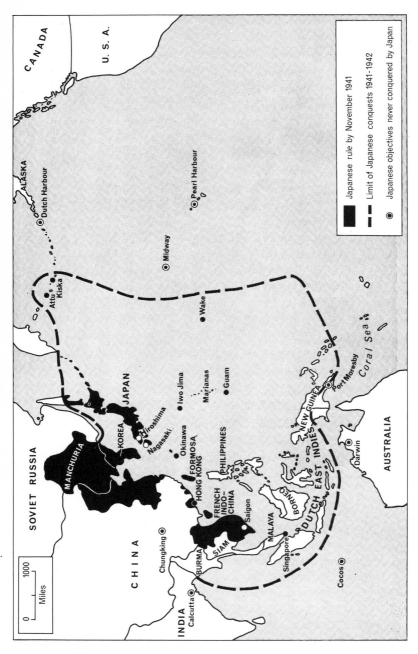

The Far East, 1941

Legend:
- Japanese rule by November 1941
- Limit of Japanese conquests 1941-1942
- Japanese objectives never conquered by Japan

CANADA
U.S.A.
ALASKA
Dutch Harbour
SOVIET RUSSIA
MANCHURIA
KOREA
JAPAN
Hiroshima
Nagasaki
Okinawa
FORMOSA
HONG KONG
FRENCH INDO-CHINA
Saigon
CHINA
Chungking
BURMA
SIAM
MALAYA
Singapore
Calcutta
INDIA
BORNEO
DUTCH EAST INDIES
PHILIPPINES
Iwo Jima
Marianas
Guam
Wake
Midway
Pearl Harbour
Attu
Kiska
NEW GUINEA
Port Moresby
Coral Sea
Darwin
AUSTRALIA
Cocos

0   1000
Miles

peace. The argument for war therefore prevailed.

During the night of 4–5 December 1941 the German army in Russia reached the suburbs of Moscow. That night the temperature fell ot —63° Fahrenheit, the coldest night for more than a hundred years. The horsemeat which formed the main item of German diet was frozen too hard to cut with an axe. Hot soup froze solid before the bowl could be finished. That night the Russians, under General Zhukov, launched a massive counter-attack. The Germans were thrown back in chaos. It was their first setback in nearly two years of war. That same night, on the other side of Asia, secretly, stealthily, and with aggressive intent, Japanese aircraft carriers were steaming across the Pacific. Their orders were to strike without warning at the principal United States air and sea base at Pearl Harbor.

On the morning of 7 December the Japanese reached their destination. Within an hour of the first Japanese air strike nearly half of America's Pacific fleet was crippled. At the same moment other Japanese planes struck at the American bases in Wake and Guam, and at British military positions in Hong Kong and Malaya. The war in Asia had begun.

The Japanese conquests were rapid. Britain's only two battle-ships in the Far East, the *Prince of Wales* and the *Repulse,* were sunk by aircraft on 10 December. Two weeks later Hong Kong was occupied by Japan. Thailand at once accepted Japanese domination. The Philippines surrendered in January, Malaya in February, the Dutch East Indies in March, Burma in May. By July 1942 Japanese control in the Pacific extended in a great semi-circle with a radius of over 3,000 miles. India, Australia and Alaska were within bombing range of Japanese planes.

Hitler was full of admiration for Japan's success. He believed that the United States would never recover its strength or courage. He therefore immediately declared war on the United States. It was an error as serious as his invasion of Russia, perhaps more so. The vast military might of the United States was now geared to war. The lull in American preparedness was over. American hesitations were at an end. Hitler failed to realize that Roosevelt would unite and mobilize the American people, who would create a war machine capable of destroying both the German and Japanese Empires.

At the very moment when the United States was preoccupied with Japan, and might be expected to focus all her effort on the

1942: Japanese soldiers cheer their victory. In six months they had conquered the Philippines, Malaya, Burma, the Dutch East Indies and most of the western Pacific.

war in the Pacific, Hitler forced Roosevelt to turn half of that effort against Germany. By this foolish gesture, Hitler, already disastrously entangled in Russia, made his defeat inevitable.

The American people had not sought war with Japan. For four years they refrained from military action in support of China. Nor were they entirely hostile to Japan's search for a south-east Asian 'Co-Prosperity Sphere'. They were, indeed, strongly critical of the British, French and Dutch Empires, regarding them as unjust impositions of alien rule. They had listened with some sympathy to the cry of 'Asia for the Asians', but they looked with less favour on the Japanese goal, 'Asia for the Japanese'.

The treachery of the Pearl Harbor attack was decisive. Until then the American people were divided in their attitudes to military aggression, and uncertain of where America ought to stand. Pearl Harbor made up their minds for them. Roosevelt, speaking on the radio two days later, found himself speaking to a united people. 'The sources of international brutality,' he declared, 'wherever they exist, must be absolutely and finally broken.' He explained that the United States was not entering the war for any material gain: 'The true goal we seek is far above and beyond the ugly field of battle. . . . We are now in the midst of a war, not for conquest, not for vengeance, but for a world in which this nation, and all that this nation represents, will be safe for our children.'

Roosevelt told the American people that although the war would be a long and savage one, he was confident of final victory. Across the Atlantic, Churchill was equally confident that, with the United States fully committed to war, Hitler, Mussolini and Hirohito, would all be defeated. When the war was over, he recalled his feelings on hearing of the Japanese attack on Pearl Harbor: 'No American will think it wrong of me if I proclaim that to have the United States at our side was to me the greatest joy. I could not foretell the course of events. I do not pretend to have measured accurately the martial might of Japan, but now at this very moment I knew the United States was in the war, up to the neck and in to the death. So we had won after all! . . . after seventeen months of lonely fighting and nineteen months of my responsibility in dire distress. We had won the war. England would live; Britain would live; the Commonwealth of Nations and the Empire would live. How long the war would last or in what fashion it would end no man could tell, nor did I at this moment care. Once again in our long Island history we should emerge, however mauled or mutilated, safe and victorious. We should not be wiped out. Our history would not come to an end. . . . Hitler's fate was sealed. Mussolini's fate was sealed. As for the Japanese, they would be ground to powder. All the rest was merely the proper application of overwhelming force.'

12

Global War

BETWEEN 1939 and 1941 three major powers, the United States, Russia and Japan, had stood outside the ring of nations at war. By January 1942 each of these three powers was deeply involved in the conflict. They were each, in Churchill's phrase, 'at death-grips with events'. Their future depended upon the outcome of the war. Soviet Communism could only survive if Germany were defeated. The struggle between Japan and the United States would decide whether south-east Asia was to be exploited by an imperial overlord, or be free to choose its own economic and political destiny. The control of the wide expanses of the Pacific Ocean was also at stake.

German-occupied Europe was now part of a much wider war which involved new issues, and was directed by new men. For over a year Britain had stood alone, overcoming fear, symbolizing courage, upholding the rights of free men everywhere. During that time Churchill showed extraordinary pluck and skill. But now both his own genius and that of the British whom he led were to be eclipsed by, and subordinated to other aims and other needs. Stalin, Roosevelt and their advisers were eager to press forward with their own plans. They admired what Britain had achieved. But they had interests of their own.

Russia, Britain and the United States were now, in theory, allies. Each was at war with Germany. Britain and the United States were also at war with Japan. But these three powers had not worked together in harmony since the First World War, twenty-five years before. Even then, their co-operation had not lasted very long or been very close. Now they had to try to work together. It was not an easy task.

On 1 January 1942, with twenty-three other nations, Britain, Russia and the United States signed in Washington a United Nations Declaration. This created an official allied coalition. It was the largest wartime coalition ever formed. Yet its aims were diverse and its disagreements many. One decision it did reach, and keep. Each of the twenty-six nations agreed not to make a separate peace with Germany, Italy or Japan. They would devote their full economic and military power against the enemy. And they would all fight to the finish.

There was otherwise little unity of aims among the allies. Britain wanted to re-establish the independence of the states in eastern Europe which Hitler had conquered. It was for Poland's independence that Britain went to war in 1939. But Russia preferred to see those states turned into a communist buffer zone protecting Russia from the capitalist West. The United States favoured the rise of independent states in south-east Asia once the Japanese were defeated. Roosevelt did not like the idea of fighting Japanese imperialism only to restore European imperialism. Britain, France and Holland, however, wished to re-establish their rule in Asia after the defeat of Japan.

Equally serious disagreements arose over the question of the future of Germany. Even within Governments there was division on this. Some people wanted to crush Germany for all time. They believed that Europe's future security would depend upon a weak, even a divided Germany. They wanted to destroy all German industry and put the German people permanently to farming and agriculture. Others remembered that it was German bitterness after the defeat of 1918 which helped Hitler on his rise to power. They argued in favour of leniency to Germany once Hitler and the leading Nazis had been defeated. Many people in the United States hoped to defeat Japan before Germany. But the British wanted the defeat of Germany to be given priority.

These deep differences of opinion were discussed at over twenty-five major allied conferences, held all over the world. Churchill was particularly active. He met Roosevelt eight and Stalin four times. For a man of nearly seventy these frequent, long and tiring journeys, mostly by air, were a remarkable achievement. As a result of this, the British view often prevailed. At Washington in January 1942 the United States agreed to concentrate on the defeat of Germany and Italy before launching an all-out assault on Japan. At Casablanca in January 1943 Roosevelt and Churchill agreed that the war should go on until the 'unconditional surrender' of Germany. This meant that at no stage would the allies agree to any 'bargain' in return for peace. Germany was to be destroyed, not used by the capitalist west in any future conflict against Communist Russia.

One disagreement caused continued ill-feeling after 1941.

The Big Three: Roosevelt and Stalin celebrate Churchill's sixty-ninth birthday during the Teheran Conference in November 1943. Roosevelt had travelled 7,000 miles, Churchill 4,000 and Stalin 1,500 miles to discuss war policy.

Less than a month after the German invasion of Russia, Stalin wrote to Churchill that 'the military situation of the Soviet Union, as well as of Great Britain, would be considerably improved if there could be established a front against Hitler in the west—northern France. . . .' This Soviet demand for a 'Second Front' was often repeated in the next two years. It was vigorously supported by some British newspapers and Members of Parliament. But Britain was already fighting the Germans both in north Africa and on the Atlantic Ocean. It did not have the men or weapons to launch an invasion of northern France. This was an area well-defended by the Germans, who had built strong fortified positions along the whole Channel Coast, which only a major, full-scale, inter-allied attack could breach. But Stalin insisted on an immediate Second Front. It was, he argued, the only effective way to help relieve the pressure of German troops in the east.

Churchill went to Moscow in August 1941 in order to explain to Stalin why Britain could not open a Second Front in 1942. It was not until May 1943 that Roosevelt and Churchill, meeting

in Washington, fixed mid-1944 as the date for the invasion of
Normandy. Stalin complained bitterly that this was not soon
enough. But it was the earliest possible moment for Britain and
the United States. The Battle of the Atlantic and the war in
north Africa had to be won first. Germany's oil reserves had to be
weakened. German war production had to be reduced. German
morale had, if possible, to be shaken.

December 1943: bombs fall on German U-boat base at Toulon during a British
   bombing raid. Part of the waterfront is already ablaze.

For these objectives a full-scale bombing offensive was launched
early in 1942. German cities, as well as factories, bridges and oil
refineries, were bombed with increasing severity for over two
years. At Hamburg 50,000 people were killed in two nights, at
Cologne 14,000 people in one night, at Darmstadt 12,000, at
Bremerhaven 10,000, at Kassel 8,000 in a single night raid. We
now know that these raids broke neither the morale nor the
industrial power of Germany. But at the time they were thought

to be an indispensable prelude, first to invasion, then to victory.

Up to June 1942 Germany and Japan advanced quickly, over vast distances. They gained control of immense areas. They obtained all the war material they needed from within their own Empires. They used the forced labour of their many captive peoples to increase their war production. They ensured the obedience of those they ruled by terror and reprisals. But these achievements signified little. In reality, Germany and Japan had conquered a wider area than they could control. They had brought upon themselves a larger coalition of enemies than they could ever defeat. Yet their enemies had made it clear that they would accept no compromise, no barter, no negotiations. Deprived of victory, the Germans, Italians and Japanese had no alternative but to fight on until they were defeated. It might take many years. It would certainly cost many lives. But it could not be averted.

13

Behind Enemy Lines

THE occupied nations of Europe and Asia did not lie tamely under German or Japanese rule. Conquest did not imply automatic co-operation and the end of all fighting. In Indo-China Ho Chi-minh, who had once been a pastry cook in London, organized a resistance movement which fought the Japanese tenaciously for four years. The United States gave him their support. He, in his turn, sheltered American pilots who had been shot down by the Japanese. In Malaya and the Philippines resistance movements were also active in sabotaging Japanese military installations and stealing Japanese supplies. These movements were mostly communist-led. This was welcomed by the United States and Britain, for Russia was then their ally.

Some Asians collaborated with the Japanese, particularly in Burma and Indonesia. The Japanese still spoke up as the champions of Asian freedom from white domination. As a result they won a certain support among those who were already anti-western and anti-imperialist. But the Japanese soon began to use the wealth of their captives entirely for their own war effort. They abandoned their earlier, more attractive claim to be the founders of the New Order of the Greater East Asia Co-Prosperity Sphere. They also committed frequent atrocities against their European prisoners-of-war. They tortured and starved and put to slave labour the British soldiers captured when Malaya and Burma had surrendered. Such actions aroused Asian hostility. Asians might dislike white rule. But they liked Japanese savagery even less.

Despite the grave risks attached to resistance, anti-Japanese activity grew steadily throughout south-east Asia. By the end of 1944, for example, Ho Chi-minh was directing a guerrilla campaign successful enough for the United States to parachute in both arms and advisers.

European resistance movements followed a similar pattern. They did not grow everywhere. In a number of countries German rule or influence was not too severe. In places the Germans were able to set up 'puppet' regimes. In Slovakia, Croatia, Vichy France and Norway there were many local people who accepted German rule as inevitable. Some were too afraid, others too complacent to fight against it. The Germans encouraged such collaboration as much as possible. They wanted a quiet life in occupied areas. They even hoped to be able to set up a 'quisling' government in Britain, once they had conquered it.

But resistance is not so easily snuffed out. Throughout Europe there were people for whom Nazism was too odious for there to be any compromise with it.

German brutality grew as the war progressed. It surpassed in scale the brutality of any nation in the First World War, in the Napoleonic wars and in most earlier medieval wars. Above all, it signified a reversal of recent progress in matters of warfare. All war is cruel. But after the Crimean War of 1854 men felt the need to set a limit to the cruelties committed in war. Two Conventions, held at Geneva in 1864 and 1929, laid down clear laws about the treatment of enemy wounded, and civilians, in occupied areas. Enemy wounded could no longer be left to die on the battlefield once the battle was over, or killed as they lay helpless on the ground. Civilians were protected against reprisals and soldiers were forbidden to terrorize them. The United States did not sign the Geneva Conventions. But Britain and Germany were among the many states which did. Both were therefore bound by their signature to treat civilians in occupied areas humanely. Three years after the 1929 Convention, Hitler came to power. He encouraged the German people to turn against liberalism, tolerance and decency between men. Ten years after signing the Convention, German soldiers began, flagrantly and systematically, to break it. The Nazi Government deliberately turned its back on the earlier German decision to limit the evils of warfare. By so doing, it showed that the civilized world could easily sink to barbarism.

The ranks of the many different partisan groups increased with each German atrocity. In June 1942, as a reprisal against the murder in Czechoslovakia of a leading Nazi, German troops surrounded the Czech village of Lidice. The village had no connection at all with the murder. No one was allowed to leave. A twelve-year-old boy who tried to run off was shot dead. The next day the Germans killed all the men and boys over sixteen, 172 in all. The 195 women and 83 children were sent to a concentration camp. 52 of the women were killed. This was not an isolated example of German terror. Reprisals of this sort were frequent in Poland, Russia, Greece and Yugoslavia. In France, at Oradour-sur-Glane, a village was suspected of hiding ammunition. As a reprisal 245 women, 207 children and 190 men were killed. Only nine men and one woman survived.

All these actions were grotesque. Yet they took place all over Europe. In Poland, Greece, Czechoslovakia and Yugoslavia, by the end of the war, many more civilians had been killed than soldiers. One result of these repeated atrocities was that the resistance movements grew rapidly. In France, Russia and Yugoslavia large areas of the countryside fell almost entirely under partisan rule. Germans dared not walk alone. Even small, well-armed groups were likely to be attacked. German trains were seldom able to go far without being derailed. In Denmark such sabotage was particularly effective.

Wherever German troops tried to cow the local population, brave men and women were willing to risk death in order to oppose them. The allies did whatever was possible to help resistance. Arms and food were parachuted into partisan territory. British agents made contact with partisans in Norway, Greece, Yugoslavia, Italy and Albania. Radio contact was maintained with allied headquarters. Sabotage was co-ordinated with allied raids.

1942: a Jewish boy surrenders to the Germans in the Warsaw Ghetto. The
Germans killed over five million Jewish men, women and children as a
deliberate attempt to destroy the Jews altogether.

The partisans of Europe were courageous men and women.
They knew that the Germans would show no mercy if they were
caught. Sometimes the local people with whom they hid turned
against them. For it was not only dangerous to be a partisan. It
was equally dangerous to help one. In December 1943 Hitler
issued an order which encouraged the Germans to use brutality
in fighting partisans. The order was everywhere obeyed. It read
as follows:

'If the repression of bandits in the east, as well as in the Balkans, is not pursued by the most brutal means, the forces at our disposal will, before long, be insufficient to exterminate this plague. The troops, therefore, have the right and the duty to use any means, even against women and children, provided they are conducive to success. Scruples of any sort are a crime against the German people and against the German soldiers. . . . No German participating in action against bandits and their associates is to be held responsible for acts of violence either from a disciplinary or a judicial point of view.'

As a result of this order, reprisals increased in intensity. In White Russia alone over a million people are thought to have died during the partisan war. There were other causes of civilian deaths. In early 1942 Hitler decided to murder as many Jews as possible. In 1937 there had been less than half a million Jews in Germany. But as a result of German conquests, over seven million lived inside the Greater Germany of 1942. These were now marked out for death.

For two years the Germans organized the systematic murder of European Jewry. From every occupied country the Jews were sent to concentration camps set up in Germany or Poland. Here they were starved, beaten, put to forced labour, and, finally, gassed or shot. By the end of 1944 over five million had been killed.

Often the local inhabitants tried to shield the Jews from death. In Holland a general strike took place in 1941 which temporarily prevented all deportation. In Denmark all the resources of a plucky people led to the whole Jewish population, seven thousand, being ferried secretly to neutral Sweden, and to safety. All over Europe monasteries and convents hid as many Jews as they could, although the penalty for shielding a Jew was death.

The Jews themselves rebelled wherever possible. In a number of towns and concentration camps they staged full-scale uprisings. But the Germans were all-powerful in Europe. Every challenge to German rule led to savage reprisals. Most acts of self-defence were in vain. Even so, many Jews escaped death by their own efforts. In German-occupied Russia they formed their own Jewish partisan band. In France they set up a special resistance group. In Warsaw they rose up against the Germans, and fought fiercely for many days. Their resistance was a noble chapter in a sordid war. But once again German power prevailed.

Hitler's Europe, 1942

It was not the Germans alone who murdered Jews. In Odessa, Rumanian soldiers murdered 25,000 Jews by machine-gun fire. Anti-Jewish atrocities were carried out by Hungarians, Ukrainians, Croats, Latvians and Slovaks. The German mastery of Europe provided a cloak for many acts of terror by those who were at heart as cruel as any German could be, and had earlier lacked only the opportunity for violence. The catalogue of anti-Jewish crimes is long and horrible. But non-Jewish deaths were even higher, and equally terrible.

All killing is an insult to human intelligence, and a negation of every spiritual and humanistic ethic. In war soldiers expect to die. But the murder of children who cannot resist, of their parents who have been starved and beaten beyond all endurance, these have no justification. The Second World War saw barbarism triumph in Europe. No one can read of these events without realizing the dangers inherent in human society. For many years Europe led the world in culture, science, philosophy and medicine. For five years it led the world in murder.

14

Roads to Victory: The Pacific

THE Germans and the Japanese both reached the limit of their military expansion by mid-1942. Neither possessed the power to advance farther east. The Germans never reached the Urals. The Japanese never set foot on Hawaii. Pearl Harbor, the scene of the first Japanese air onslaught, was held by the United States throughout the war.

Both Germany and Japan fell after 1942 into four grave difficulties, which prevented them from advancing farther. These difficulties also made it increasingly hard for them to control the territory already under their rule. First, neither was able to stop the mounting scale of partisan activity. Second, neither could control the oceans sufficiently to prevent the mass movement of allied troops and supplies. Third, neither held control of the air, with the result that allied planes could guard and search and bomb over an ever-growing area. Fourth, and perhaps of greatest importance, neither Japan nor Germany could obtain the oil they needed, or halt the flow of oil to the allied powers.

Oil is of major importance in modern warfare. Tanks, trucks and cars depend upon it. Ships and submarines are driven by it. Aircraft cannot fly without it. Any nation which seeks to conquer must be certain that it can get oil easily and without interruption. Any nation intending to defeat an enemy or drive out an occupation must likewise depend upon an adequate supply of oil.

It was in order to have their own source of oil that Japan had invaded the Dutch East Indies and Germany had obtained control over Rumania. Neither was able to interfere with the main sources of allied oil, Texas, Venezuela, the Caucasus and the Persian Gulf. But they were able to attack allied oil tankers on their slow, long, exposed journeys from the oilfields to the ports of Britain, India and Australia. Some attacks were by air. Most were by submarine. But the tankers continued on their perilous paths. Despite many sinkings, sufficient oil reached the war zones to keep the allied vehicles and planes in full supply.

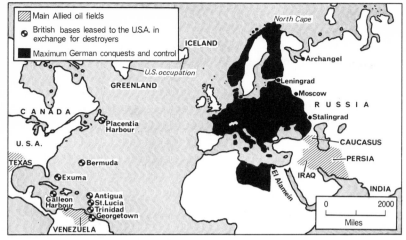

Allied Power, 1942

No such fortune favoured Germany or Japan. Their supplies were not as large as those of the allies. And the routes by which they had to travel were equally exposed to attack. As allied air power increased, one of its major tasks was to break the smooth flow of oil into Germany and Japan.

At the height of their power, Germany and Japan could only produce 120 million barrels of oil a year. The total allied production was over 2,000 million barrels, most of it from Texas. In June 1944, when the allies obtained absolute air mastery over Europe, they launched as their first priority an 'Oil Campaign'. Within six weeks over three-quarters of Germany's oil reserves and production were destroyed.

The allies could move only slowly against Japan. In April 1942 the Japanese fleet and air force were intact. Their men were based on a thousand Pacific Islands. Each island was fortified. The Japanese were confident that they could not be dislodged. But Japan was not content with holding the vast areas already under its control. The military leaders wished to advance still farther. Plans were made to invade Australia, and to occupy the American base on Midway Island. By failing to see the limits of secure conquest, Japan put its head into a noose. The attack on Australia was stopped by the Americans in the Battle of the Coral Sea in May. The losses on both sides were severe. But Japan was deprived of its objective.

Shortly before the war American intelligence had succeeded in breaking the Japanese code system. They were therefore able to intercept and read secret messages sent out from Tokyo to the fleet. As a result they learnt in advance of the Japanese decision to conquer Midway Island. They also knew exactly when and where this attack would come. When it did, they were ready. After a fierce battle, Midway Island remained in American hands. Four Japanese aircraft carriers were sunk, and Japanese naval predominance in the Pacific destroyed.

From that moment Japan never regained the initiative. Slowly, and with terrible slaughter on both sides, American ships and soldiers edged their way closer and closer towards Japan. Over the Pacific American planes, after heavy losses, won almost full control. With each advance, new airbases could be used from which to move air attacks nearer and nearer to Japan. At Leyte Gulf, in October 1944, the Japanese fleet suffered its second severe defeat. With the capture of Iwo Jima island in March 1945, the Americans were able to bomb Japanese cities as often as they chose to do so. As in every Pacific battle, there was much hand-to-hand fighting at Iwo Jima, and scenes of indescribable horror.

Iwo Jima was a tiny island, hardly large enough for three runways, alongside each other. But as an airfield its capture was vital to victory. 5,000 U.S. marines were killed in capturing it. 20,000 Japanese died in defending it. In April 1945 the capture of a second island, Okinawa, gave the Americans an airbase even closer to Japan. Over 100,000 Japanese were killed before it was captured. 11,000 American soldiers died in the attack. The Japanese had been driven back 3,000 miles across the Pacific to within 350 miles of Japan itself.

The United States now controlled the Pacific Ocean. No Japanese city escaped being bombed. The Japanese realized that they had lost the war. The Emperor was anxious to make peace. But those who wanted a 'war to the finish', even if it meant total defeat, still controlled Japan. The Emperor's wishes were ignored. The war went on. More and more Japanese cities were burned and blasted by the American air force. Half a million Japanese civilians died in the holocaust.

The final Japanese strategy was a bizarre one. Japanese pilots were formed into special attack squadrons called 'Kamikaze'. Their task was to crash their planes deliberately on to the decks of American ships. Each plane was filled with explosives. These suicide dives brought death and confusion to the Americans, who

April 1945: American marines armed with flame-throwers advance on Japanese positions in Iwo Jima.

had over a thousand ships bringing hundreds of thousands of men, and tons of oil and supplies, across the Pacific to the fighting zones.

Before leaving Japan the Kamikaze pilots attended their own funeral, and sent farewell letters to their parents: 'Please do not weep because I am about to die,' wrote one. 'I do not want a grave. I would feel oppressed if they were to put me in a narrow vault,' wrote another. 'May our death be as sudden and clean as the shattering of crystal,' asked a third. These self-inflicted individual deaths led to great slaughter. In April 1945, at Okinawa, over 3,500 Kamikaze pilots dived towards American ships. 10,000 American sailors were killed or wounded, the highest casualties in any period of American naval history. Thirty-six ships were sunk and about 400 damaged. A Japanese air observer broadcast live an account of a Kamikaze attack for the people of Japan:

'The leading Kamikaze dives, dropping vertically into a barbed-wire entanglement of anti-aircraft fire. He'll never make

A Japanese suicide pilot crashes his plane into an America aircraft carrier. In one month over 3,500 suicide pilots plunged to their deaths. But only 36 American ships were sunk.

the aircraft carriers; that seems obvious. Instead, he's heading for a cruiser near the fringe. For a moment it looks as if he'll make it. But no—he's hit, and its all over. His plane is a red flare, fading, dropping from sight.

'Everything is a blur now—a mixture of sound and colour. Two more of them go the same way, exploding in mid-air. A fourth is luckier. He screams unscathed through the barrage, levelling inside the anti-aircraft fire's umbrella near the water. A hit! He's struck a destroyer right at the waterline. A bellowing explosion, then another and another. It's good! It's good! The ship is in its death throes. . . .

'Tatsuno is alone now, still unhit, making a perfect run, better than they ever taught us in school. Tatsuno! Tatsuno! Fire spouts from his tail section, but he keeps going. The orange fingers reach out. His plane is a moving sheet of flame, but they can't stop him. Tatsuno! A tanker looms, ploughing the leaden liquid. They're closing! A hit! An enormous explosion rocks the atmosphere. For a curious instant embers seem to roll and dance. Now a staccato series of smaller bursts and one mighty blast, shaking the sea like a blanket. The tanker is going down. Gone. No trace but the widening shroud of oil.'

The Kamikazes could not halt the advance of American power. The bombing of Japan increased in intensity. On 9 March 1945 three hundred and thirty-four American planes flew over Tokyo. It was night-time. Their aim was to set as much of the capital on fire as possible. In this they succeeded. Sixteen square miles of the most densely populated city in Asia were reduced to rubble and ashes. No American planes were shot down in the raid. Fourteen were lost at sea. Over 83,000 Japanese were killed. The war had everywhere become a holocaust. Neither soldiers nor civilians escaped the worst torments which civilized man could devise.

15

Roads to Victory: Europe

In October 1942 the British defeated the combined German and Italian armies at El Alamein. They drove them back across the desert from Egypt to Tunisia. At the same time American troops landed in force in north Africa and advanced towards Tunis from the west. The German and Italian troops were trapped.

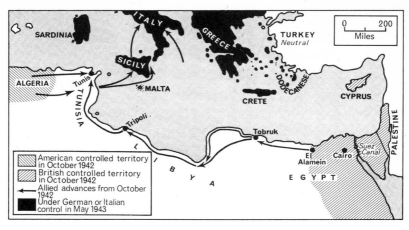

North Africa, 1942

Hundreds of thousands of them surrendered. The allies crossed into Sicily and then, elated by their success, invaded Italy itself.

The Italians were weary of war. They had been told often enough about 'glory', 'conquest', 'sacrifice', and other fine-sounding virtues. But the invasion of Italy brought to a climax their distaste of fascism and their fear of fierce fighting in their own towns and cities. Almost immediately after the first allied landings, Italy surrendered. An anti-German Government came to power. Mussolini found refuge in northern Italy, where Hitler put him at the head of yet another 'puppet' Government. Like Pavelic in Croatia, Quisling in Norway and Pétain in France, he could now do very little unless Hitler told him to.

The allies advanced northwards through Italy. The Germans quickly occupied Milan and Rome. For two years the allied forces—Americans, Britons, Poles, among them—advanced northwards. The fighting was fierce, and allied progress slow. In October 1943 the allies entered Naples. In June 1944, after a difficult campaign, Rome was liberated from German rule.

In June 1944 the long-awaited 'Second Front' was opened. The allies landed in Normandy. The Germans were caught unprepared. Allied air control was absolute. On the day of the invasion the Germans could get no more than 300 planes into the air. The British and Americans could send up at will 5,000 fighters and 5,000 bombers. The Germans were soon in retreat. Their lack of oil prevented the rapid movement of adequate reinforcements to the battle area.

1942: the allies drive the Germans and Italians out of Africa. 500,000 men surrendered; here the prisoners-of-war are gathered together in vast camps.

The allies had laid an oil pipe-line under the Channel from
Britain to France. For them, oil flowed in abundance. Troops
advanced rapidly, and in great numbers. The Germans had
400,000 men to meet the invading army. By July, the allies had
landed over 1,600,000. This superiority was decisive. Cherbourg
was liberated on 27 July; Paris on 24 August. The Americans

June 1944: American troops wade ashore from their landing-craft during the D-Day landings in Normandy.

reached the German frontier on 12 September. The liberation of western Europe was almost complete.

It was on the Russian front that fighting was most severe. For nearly three years the Germans threatened Leningrad, Stalingrad and Moscow. Only in late 1943 were the Russians able to make deep advances. Already two or three million Russians soldiers were dead. Another two million were to die before the war was over. A third of these were killed, not on the field of battle, but in German death camps. The Germans treated Russian prisoners-of-war as vermin. Few survived.

It has often been argued that for three years the British and Americans left the task of killing Germans to the Soviet Union. During that period the Russians fought and repulsed 180 German divisions, while in north Africa and Italy only ten German divisions held up the Anglo-American armies. It is true that over 85 per cent of the Germans who died fighting were killed on the Russian front. For the Russians, these figures have been a

June 1944: reinforcements and supplies roll on to the beach-head after the allied Normandy landing.

frequent cause of bitterness. They point out that whereas only 130,000 Americans died in Europe, Russian deaths were over five million. But in fact, each ally pursued what it felt were the most useful policies to win the war, and each played an effective part.

Germany finally lost the war on the Russian front. When the western allies crossed the Rhine in March 1945 the Russians had already crossed the Oder. The western allies had driven the Germans from north Africa, France and Italy. The Russians had driven them from Russia, Rumania, Bulgaria, Hungary, Yugoslavia, Poland, Czechoslovakia, Prussia and Silesia.

But in the last months of the war the Russian motive was not entirely military. Stalin's aim was to control as much territory as possible west of Russia. In almost all the countries occupied by his armies, he soon established communist regimes which he hoped to be able to control for many years. In the west, no such political considerations were at work. The United States and Britain had no desire to set up 'puppet' governments. Their sole aim was to defeat Nazism.

1945: on the Russian front two members of a German tank crew are boys. In October 1944 sixteen became the official age for the start of military service in Germany.

Much of the allied success arose from skilful bombing. Before the Normandy landings they attacked the bridges and railway yards in northern France along which German reinforcements

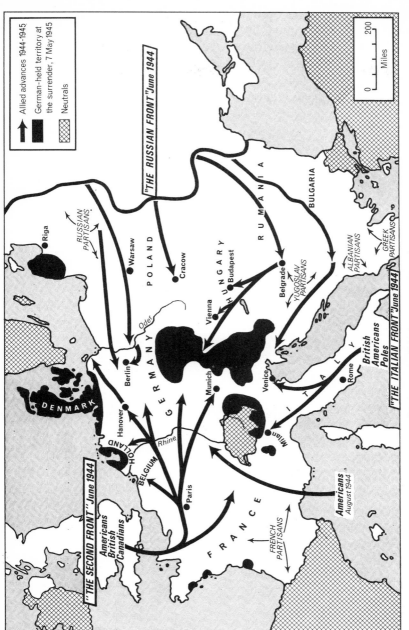

The Defeat of Germany, 1944–1945

Legend:

- Allied advances 1944–1945
- German-held territory at the surrender, 7 May 1945
- Neutrals

200 Miles

"THE RUSSIAN FRONT" June 1944

"THE SECOND FRONT" June 1944

"THE ITALIAN FRONT" June 1944

Americans
British
Canadians

Americans
August 1944

British
Americans
Poles

RUSSIAN PARTISANS

RUMANIA

BULGARIA

Riga

Warsaw

POLAND

Cracow

HUNGARY

Vienna

Budapest

Belgrade

YUGOSLAV PARTISANS

ALBANIAN PARTISANS

GREEK PARTISANS

DENMARK

Berlin

Oder

G E R M A N Y

Munich

Venice

Rome

I T A L Y

Milan

Hanover

HOLLAND

Rhine

BELGIUM

Paris

F R A N C E

FRENCH PARTISANS

had to come. After the landings they at once destroyed Germany's oil reserves. Allied bombers crippled the German aircraft industry. They put hundreds of factories out of operation. Sometimes they exaggerated the effect of this 'strategic' bombing. But it was certainly a major asset to the armies advancing on Germany both from east and west.

There was, however, a second bombing policy. This aimed at killing as many German civilians as possible. The targets were crowded cities. The weapons were fire-bombs. These created whirlwinds of flame against which water-hoses were in vain. These 'fire-raids' began in 1942. As a result, hundreds of German towns were in ruins by January 1945, and millions of people without homes. The aim of this 'terror bombing' was to frighten and demoralize the German people. Instead, it probably stiffened their resolve to continue at war.

The 'terror bombing' reached its climax on the night of 13 February 1945. That night British bombers made two attacks on Dresden. The citizens of this fine medieval city believed that they would not be bombed for as long as Oxford, its English equivalent, remained intact. Oxford was never bombed. But no such agreement ever existed. Dresden was full of German refugees fleeing from the advancing Russians.

The city burned all night. No one knows how many people were killed in the holocaust. The Germans were still trying to count the charred remains when the Russians arrived two weeks later. Certainly 40,000 people were killed. Possibly over 100,000. Churchill was so shocked when he heard what had happened that he ordered an immediate halt to 'terror bombing'. But the damage was done. In three years, over half a million German civilians had been killed. It is doubtful whether this slaughter in any way helped bring the war to an early end.

During the last year of the war in Europe the allied leaders saw little of each other. But they exchanged hundreds of letters and sent hundreds of telegrams. By January 1945 they were fully agreed on how to win the war. Bombing continued over Germany. On all fronts their vast, reinforced armies advanced. But the allied leaders quarrelled over the nature of the peace which was to follow.

In February 1945 the 'Big Three', Roosevelt, Churchill and Stalin, met at Yalta on the Russian Black Sea coast. Here they faced each other over grave differences of policy. It became clear

February 1945: after a single night raid by British bombers, the city of Dresden was destroyed and over 100,000 Germans are thought to have died. Many were refugees fleeing from the advancing Russians. This photograph shows the main shopping centre of the city. American planes also took part in the raid.

1945: three American soldiers advance through the ruins of a German city.

at once that Stalin's view of peacetime Europe was almost unalterable. He wanted Russia to be protected by a 'buffer zone' of small Communist states stretching from the Baltic to the Adriatic. He intended to set up these regimes, if necessary, by the strength of his armies. He wanted Poland, Bulgaria and Rumania to be under his control. He hoped to see Communism spread also to Yugoslavia, Czechoslovakia, Albania and parts of Germany. Churchill persuaded him to leave Greece in the 'western' orbit. But that was Stalin's only concession.

Neither Roosevelt nor Churchill could prevent Stalin from having his way, for Russian troops were already masters of almost all eastern Europe. They had liberated its inhabitants from Nazi rule. They had won the victor's laurels. Stalin did not intend to withdraw. Churchill feared the 'Bolshevization' of Europe. But Britain did not have the power to challenge Russia.

Roosevelt wanted to exclude France from a share in the occupation of Germany. He enlisted Stalin's support. But Churchill insisted, successfully, that France should also be treated as a 'victor' nation, even though the French Government at Vichy had collaborated with the Germans during the war. By Churchill's strong insistence, General de Gaulle's Free French forces, which had fought bravely on the African, Italian and Western fronts, became an accepted allied power.

The Yalta Conference issued many communiqués on the post-war future of different frontiers and countries. The 'Big Three' declared themselves in agreement over the need for democratic governments in all the liberated areas. Every people, they announced, would have the right 'to choose the form of government under which they would live'. But this was largely a sham. Neither Roosevelt nor Churchill had the power to prevent Russian control in eastern Europe. Roosevelt was entirely mistaken when he told Congress that the Yalta Conference 'ought to spell the end of the system of unilateral action, the exclusive alliances, the spheres of influence, the balances of power, and the other expedients that have been tried for centuries—and have always failed'. Churchill saw more clearly that Yalta spelt the creation of a new dictatorship over much of Europe, and a future division of the world into Communist and non-Communist states. In defence of Roosevelt, it has been argued that he was at this time a sick, and indeed a dying man. But when the war ended, his successor as President, Harry S. Truman, was equally unable, at the Potsdam Conference, to deflect Stalin from his policies.

One clear decision was reached at Yalta. This was on the future of Germany. Although it was to be occupied by the victors, it would not be permanently partitioned. Germany was to pay for some of the damage done during the war. But it was not to be crippled by debt, or turned from an industrial to an agricultural nation as many had hoped. Churchill explained this decision to the House of Commons on his return from Yalta: 'It is not the purpose of the allies to destroy the people of Germany, or to leave them without the necessary means of subsistence. Our policy is not revenge. It is to take such measures as may be necessary to secure the future peace and safety of the world. There will be a place one day for Germans in the comity of nations, but only when all traces of Nazism and militarism have been effectively and finally extirpated.'

The last phase of the war in Europe was swift and certain. On 13 February 1945, the night of the bombing of Dresden, the

Russians entered Budapest. Two months later they captured Vienna. The Americans reached Munich on 30 April. That same day Hitler committed suicide in Berlin. On 8 May the Germans surrendered unconditionally to the American, Russian, British and French representatives gathered at Rheims. The German War was over. 'The vanquished,' wrote Churchill, 'as well as the victors felt inexpressible relief. But for us in Britain and the British Empire, who had alone been in the struggle from the first day to the last and staked our existence on the result, there was a meaning beyond what even our most powerful and most valiant allies could feel. Weary and worn, impoverished but undaunted and now triumphant, we had a moment that was sublime.'

1945: German boys, after fighting in Hitler's armies, surrender to an American.

16
War and Peace

THE end of the war in Europe was not the end of suffering. There would be no more mass killing. But the evil effects of war went on. Europe was on the verge of starvation. The tyranny of Nazism was over; the tyranny of hunger had begun. The hungry and the homeless roamed the streets of every liberated city. Despair and disease were everywhere. Even in victorious Britain extra rationing had to be introduced.

In order to avert anarchy, the United States took the lead in setting up a massive aid programme. For three years they had sent weapons and instruments of death to Europe. Now they sent food and clothing. These were rushed over in massive quantities. And they arrived in time.

Aid from the United States saved Europe from famine in 1945. The Americans did even more to aleviate distress. The new President, Harry S. Truman, saw the dangers both to Europe and to the world if post-war hardship continued. 'The seeds of totalitarian regimes,' he told the United States Congress in 1947, 'are nurtured by misery and want. They spread and grow in the evil soil of poverty and strife. They reach their full growth when the hope of a people for a better life has died.' Truman was determined to keep European hopes and liberty alive. He used his country's wealth to sustain and nourish the enfeebled economies of a ravaged continent. He was supported by his Secretary of State, George Marshall, who prepared the detailed plans, and who told the world: 'Our policy is directed, not against any country or doctrine, but against hunger, poverty, desperation and chaos.'

Western Europe owed much of its rapid economic recovery to 'Marshall Aid'. The United States now stood as an active, imaginative, tolerant power, eager to bear the wide responsibilities which its leading role in the allied victory had placed upon it.

The Soviet Union was also active in Europe after its victory. By 1948 Communism dominated eastern Europe. It gained power more by threats of violence than by free votes. In ten formerly independent states Nazi terror was replaced by Communist control. The evils were fewer than they had been before. But terror remained. Secret police still imprisoned people without trial. Open criticism of the government still led to sudden arrest. Newspapers were still censored. The freedoms of speech, travel and worship were still strictly curtailed. For many millions of Europeans liberation did not bring liberty. In eastern Europe the fruits of victory were bitter and the moments of rejoicing short. There, Communism has remained the ruling creed. Until Stalin's death in 1953 it was a creed of intolerance and oppression. Since then it has modified, but only slowly.

The Second World War drove many millions of people from their homes, and from their country of origin. As refugees, they fled before the advancing armies, or sheltered in overcrowded camps without proper sanitation, clothing or food. When the war ended, every government tried to help them. But for ten years their plight remained a pitiful one. Many of the Jews who survived the mass murder of their co-religionists eventually found a home in the state of Israel, which was founded in 1948. But for thousands of other refugees there was no such Promised Land. They remained in their camps, cared for but not resettled in proper homes, the flotsam and jetsam of a cruel world. Some live there still.

As a result of their victory in Europe, the allied powers could concentrate entirely on the defeat of Japan. By May 1945 it was clear to most Japanese that defeat was near. The Japanese Government made serious efforts to open peace negotiations in June. But one obstacle stood in the way of their surrender. They wished to keep Hirohito as their Emperor. The Japanese believed that the imperial throne was the indispensable basis of all society. Without it, in their view, Japan would disintegrate. But to Truman and Churchill, the request to preserve the Emperor seemed an attempt to surrender only partially. The United States and Britain had already agreed that Japan, like Germany, must surrender unconditionally; that the allies must be allowed to determine in every detail the nature of future Japanese governments. The negotiations therefore broke down. The war went on.

On 22 July 1945 President Truman decided, with British approval, to use a new and powerful weapon against Japan. This weapon was the atom bomb. In size it was no larger than an ordinary bomb. But it had an immense destructive power. On

6 August the first atom bomb was dropped on Hiroshima. In a
few seconds 80,000 people were dead. Fearful injuries were
caused to many of those who survived. To this day the effects
of that single bomb and those few seconds are still felt, in the
forms of a sickness which come suddenly and can still lead to
death.

The Japanese Government began immediately to discuss
peacemaking. Long arguments arose in Tokyo about the terms
which they might accept. For three days these discussions continued. Despite the terrible suffering of the past year, surrender
seemed almost impossible for a nation which had achieved so
much, advanced so far, conquered so many. While discussions
continued in Tokyo, news was brought that a second atom bomb
had been dropped on Nagasaki. Again, only a single bomb and a
few seconds; but another 40,000 Japanese were dead, and
thousands of others suffering an agony of pain.

The military leaders who had pushed Hirohito into war in
December 1941 wanted to continue even then. They argued that
there were a million Japanese soldiers still able to fight off an
American invasion. They pointed to 5,000 more Kamikaze pilots
willing to commit suicide for the Emperor. But Hirohito now
asserted himself. In the first radio broadcast which he ever made
he told his people that 'a continuation of the war will result in
the ultimate collapse and obliteration of the Japanese nation'.
On 14 August 1945 the Japanese Government offered to surrender.
On 2 September peace was signed on board an American battle-
ship in Tokyo Bay. The world was at peace. Over 30 million
soldiers and civilians had been killed in five years.

The atom bomb changed the nature of world politics. By 1950
both the United States and Russia possessed large stocks of such
bombs, and were making the even more powerful hydrogen bomb.
These two nations had become the 'super' powers. Global war
was their decision. World peace was in their control. The other
nations could no longer dictate military solutions to the world.
Germany could no longer seek the mastery of Europe, or Japan
the mastery of south-east Asia.

Other nations could still give an important lead in culture, the
arts, medicine, literature, a way of life or an attitude of mind. But
the power to unleash death again on a scale previously impossible,
and even unthought of, lay principally with Russia and the
United States. Despite deep differences of opinions and many

serious quarrels, neither of these two 'super' powers has yet risked a nuclear war.

Twenty-five years have passed since the defeat of Germany and Japan. During these years world peace has been preserved. But there were nevertheless many local wars. Although restricted in the areas over which they were waged, they were not limited in the ferocity with which they were fought, nor in the suffering which they cause. In Korea in 1950, in Vietnam (formerly Indo-China) since 1964, war continued to make death and destruction a cruel commonplace of the twentieth century. 1945 was the year of Victory. But it was not the year of Peace.

For Further Reading

GENERAL BACKGROUND

A. L. C. Bullock, *Hitler: A Study in Tyranny.* Odhams and Penguin.

James MacGregor Burns, *Roosevelt: The Lion and the Fox.* Harcourt Brace & World Inc.

Winston S. Churchill, *The Second World War.* Cassell.

Isaac Deutscher, *Stalin.* O.U.P. and Penguin.

Martin Gilbert, *The European Powers 1900–45.* Weidenfeld & Nicolson.

T. L. Jarman, *The Rise and Fall of Nazi Germany.* Signet.

F. C. Jones, *Japan's New Order in East Asia: Its Rise and Fall 1937–45.* O.U.P.

George Kennan, *American Diplomacy 1900–50.* Secker & Warburg.

Ivone Kirkpatrick, *Mussolini.* Odhams.

Wilfrid Knapp, *A History of War and Peace 1939–65.* O.U.P.

A. J. P. Taylor, *The Origins of the Second World War.* Hamish Hamilton and Penguin.

BOOKS ON SPECIAL TOPICS

Raymond Aron, *The Vichy Regime 1940–44.* Putnam. (The story of unoccupied France)

Marc Bloch, *Strange Defeat.* Translated by Gerald Hopkins. O.U.P. (France in 1939 and 1940)

Winston S. Churchill, *Into Battle.* Cassell. (War speeches 1939 and 1940)

Alan Clark, *Barbarossa.* Hutchinson. (The German war against Russia from invasion to defeat)

Dwight D. Eisenhower, *Crusade in Europe.* Heinemann. (The American General's account of his command)

Herbert Feis, *Churchill, Roosevelt, Stalin.* O.U.P. (Wartime diplomacy in detail)

Anne Frank, *The Diary of a Young Girl.* Pan. (A Jewish girl from Holland, killed by the Germans)

Noble Frankland, *The Bombing Offensive Against Germany.* Faber. (Describes the Allied bombing of Germany)

John Hersey, *Hiroshima.* Hamish Hamilton and Penguin. (Eye-witness accounts of the first atom bomb)

David Irving, *The Destruction of Dresden*. Corgi. (British and German views of one of the severest bombing raids of the war)

John F. Kennedy, *Why England Slept*. Hutchinson. (Pre-war British policy)

W. L. Langer and S. E. Gleason, *The World Crisis and American Foreign Policy, Vol. I.: The Challenge to Isolation 1937–40*. Royal Institute of International Affairs, London. (American policy and opinion)

Ralph G. Martin, *The G.I. War*. Little, Brown & Co. (Eye-witness account of Americans on all war fronts, finely illustrated)

Viscount Montgomery, *Memoirs*. Collins. (The British General's account of his career)

William Neumann, *After Victory*. Harper Row. (Allied diplomacy during the war: the search for a just peace)

Leon Poliakov, *Harvest of Hate*. Elek. (German policy towards the Jews)

Gerald Reitlinger, *The House Built on Sand*. Weidenfeld & Nicolson. (The German occupation of Western Russia)

Telford Taylor, *The Breaking Wave*. Simon & Schuster. (Hitler's attempt to defeat Britain in 1940)

Laurence Thompson, *1940*. Collins. (Britain in the Phoney War and Blitz)

H. R. Trevor-Roper, *The Last Days of Hitler*. Macmillan. (Detailed account of Hitler's death in Berlin)

E. S. Turner, *The Phoney War on the Home Front*. Michael Joseph. (The story of British civilians in the first nine months of war)

Alexander Werth, *Russia at War*. Barrie & Rockliff. (Eye-witness accounts of heroism at the front and behind the lines)

John Wheeler-Bennett, *The Nemesis of Power: The German Army in Politics 1918–45*. Macmillan. (The detailed story of German generals and their political activity)

Index

ACROPOLIS the Swastika flies over, 54
ABYSSINIA the Italians driven out of, 50–51
ALASKA within bombing range of Japanese planes, 69
ATOM BOMB used against two Japanese cities, 100–101
AUSTRALIA within bombing range of Japanese planes, 69
AUSTRIA annexed to Germany, 14

BELGIUM German invasion of, 28; surrenders, 32
BELGRADE bombed by the Germans, 54
BONHAM CARTER Lady Violet enraged by German atrocities of 1933, 13
BRITAIN alarmed by German brutality, 13–14, frightened of German
    aggression, 15; declares war on Germany, 17; unwilling to bomb Germany,
    20; turns down German offer of peace, 23; decides to help Finland, 25;
    outnumbered in Norway, 26; debates its war failure, 28; inspired by
    Churchill's broadcasts, 31; driven out of France, 32–33; awaits a German
    invasion, 34–36; German air attacks on, 37–43; stimulated by the Greek
    resistance to Italy, 45; defeats the Italians in North Africa, 46; sends
    troops to help Greece, 54; supports Russia against Germany, 58–60; gives
    China military aid, 65; its Far Eastern possessions attacked by Japan, 69;
    allied with Russia and the United States, 72–74; bombing raids over
    German cities, 75; supports partisan activity behind German lines, 78; its
    oil supplies superior to that of Germany, 82–83; drives Germans and
    Italians from North Africa, 87; invades Italy, 88; opens Second Front in
    Normandy, 88–89; continues to bomb German cities, 94; unable to
    influence Russian post-war policy, 96–97
BURMA conquered by Japan, 69

CAIRO Mussolini hopes to ride in triumph through, 45
CASABLANCA Allied conference at decides to insist upon unconditional
    surrender of Germany, 73
CHAMBERLAIN Austen attacks German racial policies in 1933, 13–14
CHAMBERLAIN Neville British Prime Minister, 26; the demand for his
    resignation, 28; resigns, 31
CHURCHILL Winston warns against Hitler's ambitions, 15; broadcasts on
    the defeat of Poland, 21; his view of the Russian invasion of Poland, 24;
    becomes Prime Minister, 31; broadcasts about the London blitz, 42;
    supports Russia against Germany, 58–60; sees Japanese attack on United
    States as important for a final British victory, 71; travels to inter-Allied
    conferences, 73–75; at the Yalta Conference, 96–97; speaks about victory
    in Europe, 97–98
CZECHOSLOVAKIA its Bohemian, Moravian and Sudeten provinces
    incorporated in Germany, 14; Nazi atrocities in, 78; Russians drive
    Germans from, 91

DE GAULLE Charles refuses to accept French defeat, 34
DENMARK German invasion of, 26; anti-German sabotage effective in, 78;
Jews ferried to safety from, 80
DRESDEN destroyed by bombing, 94–95
DUNKIRK British and French soldiers escape from, 32
DUTCH EAST INDIES conquered by Japan, 69; provides Japan with source
of oil, 82

FINLAND Russian invasion of, 25
FRANCE willing to defend Poland against Germany, 15; declares war on
Germany, 17; German invasion of, 30; surrenders, 33; Nazi atrocities in,
78; liberated, 88–90

GERMANY its relatively weak industrial production, 7; ruled by Hitler,
11–13; its expanding frontiers, 14–15; invades Poland, 17; conquers
Poland, 18–22; invades Denmark and Norway, 26; invades Belgium,
Holland, Luxembourg and France, 28; drives British troops from France,
33; fails to conquer Britain, 34–43; dominates Europe, 46–47; conquers
Yugoslavia, 52–54; conquers Greece, 54; invades Russia, 57; fails to
conquer Russia, 62–64; at war with the United States, 69; its cities bombed
with increasing severity, 75, 94; its brutal occupation policy, 77–80; its
troops driven from North Africa, 87; in retreat in western Europe, 88;
driven from eastern Europe, 90–91; surrenders, 98
GREECE invaded by Italy, 43; defeats the Italians, 44; defeated by the
Germans, 54
GREENLAND comes under United States protection, 51

HIROHITO Emperor of Japan, 16; reluctant to go to war with the United
States, 67; agrees to war, 68; anxious to make peace, 84; makes peace, 101
HIROSHIMA atom bomb dropped on, 101
HITLER Adolf German Chancellor, 11; his methods, 12–13; his expansionist
policy, 14–15; reviews parade in conquered Warsaw, 21; his next move
after defeating Poland, 23; his policy towards Russia, 24; attacks in the
west, 28, 30; master of western Europe, 33; plans invasion of Britain,
34–37; his first defeat, 39–40; 'this wicked man', 42; his successes envied
by Mussolini, 43; his control of Europe almost complete, 47; forces the
British out of Libya, 52; invades Yugoslavia and Greece, 54; invades
Russia, 57; confident of victory over Russia, 58; realizes difficulty of
defeating Russia, 62; declares war on the United States, 69–70; orders
brutality to be used against Partisans, 79–80; commits suicide, 97–98
HO CHI-MINH organizes resistance behind Japanese lines, 76; receives
military aid from the United States, 77
HOLLAND German invasion of, 28; surrenders, 32; protects Jews, 80
HONG KONG occupied by Japan, 69

ICELAND comes under United States protection, 51
INDIA within bombing range of Japanese planes, 69
ITALY ruled by a dictator, 16; neutral at outbreak of war, 43; defeated by
the Greeks, 44; defeated by the British in North Africa, 45–46; driven out

of Abyssinia, 50–51; driven out of North Africa, 87; invaded and surrenders, 88
IWO JIMA captured by the United States, 84

JAPAN invades China, 16; advances through China, 25; its ambitions and success, 65; fails to conquer China, 66; occupies Saigon, 67; attacks United States', British and Dutch possessions in the Far East, 69–71; its policy in South East Asia, 76–77; driven from the Pacific, 83–87; opens peace negotiations, 100; makes peace, 101
JEWS Hitler reserves his greatest cruelty for, 12–14; murdered systematically throughout German-occupied Europe, 80–81; many find home in newly established State of Israel, 100

KAMIKAZE suicide pilots fail to deflect American war effort, 84–87, 101
KENNEDY John Fitzgerald believes Britain can defeat Germany, 49–50
KENNEDY Joseph sees no chance of a British victory, 49
KOREA war in, 102

LENINGRAD survives German siege, 60
LEYTE GULF Japanese fleet defeated at, 84
LIDICE Nazi atrocities in, 78
LONDON German bombing of, 40–42
LUXEMBOURG German invasion of, 28

MALAYA occupied by Japan, 69; resists Japanese rule, 76
MARSHALL George prepares plans for United States aid to post-war Europe, 99
MIDWAY ISLAND Japanese fail to conquer, 84
MOSCOW Germans fail to capture, 60
MUSSOLINI ruler of Italy, 16; seeks to emulate Hitler, 43; defeated by the Greeks, 44–45; defeated in Abyssinia, 50–51; seeks refuge in northern Italy, 88

NAGASAKI atom bomb dropped on, 101
NORMANDY Allies land in, 88–89
NORWAY German invasion of, 26

ODESSA Rumanian soldiers murder Jews in, 80
OIL its importance to the Allied victory, 82–83, 89
ORADOUR-SUR-GLANE Nazi atrocities in, 78

PANAMA CANAL closed to Japanese ships by the United States, 67
PARIS German troops march through, 33; liberated, 89
PAVELIC Ante sets up a pro-German government in Croatia, 54
PÉTAIN rules Vichy France, 34
PHILIPPINES United States territory conquered by Japan, 69; resists Japanese rule, 76
POLAND Hitler's designs upon, 15; the German invasion of, 17; conquered by Germany, 18–23; Russian action against, 24; German brutality in, 26–27

RADAR helps protect Britain from invasion, 37–38

REYNAUD Paul decides that France should fight on, 31

ROOSEVELT Franklin and the need for freedom, 17; wants to keep America out of the war, 47; decides to send Britain military aid, 47–49; confident of victory over Japan, 71; travels to inter-Allied conferences, 73; at the Yalta Conference, 96–97

RUSSIA signs treaty with Germany, 15; occupies eastern Poland, 24; attacks Finland, 25; Hitler's designs upon, 55–56; invaded by Germany, 57; determined to resist the German attack, 58; battered but unbroken, 60–64; in alliance with Britain and the United States, 72–74; resists German occupation, 80; liberates eastern Europe from German rule, 91; dominates eastern Europe after defeat of Germany, 99–100

STALIN Josef ruler of Russia, 16; makes common cause with Hitler, 24; maintains dictatorial rule, 55; ignores British warnings about invasion of Russia, 56; appeals to Britain for help, 74–75; his aims in eastern Europe, 91; dominates the Allied councils at Yalta, 94, 96–97

STALINGRAD German army defeated in streets of, 60

SUEZ CANAL Italians advance towards, 45

THAILAND (SIAM) accepts Japanese domination, 69

TOKYO bombed by 334 United States planes in one night, 87; Japanese peace discussions in, 101

TRUMAN Harry S. gives aid to post-war Europe, 99; decides to use atom bomb against Japan, 100

UNITED NATIONS DECLARATION signed in Washington, 72

UNITED STATES OF AMERICA the neutral at the beginning of the war, 47; agrees to give military aid to Britain, 48–49; escorts British ships across Atlantic, 50–51; sends military supplies to Russia, 60; sends China military aid, 65; closes Panama Canal to Japanese ships, 67; Pacific Island possessions of attacked by Japan, 69–71; drives the Japanese from the Pacific, 83–84; bombs Tokyo, 87; lands in North Africa, 87; its troops reach the German frontier, 90; gives aid to post-war Europe, 99

VERSAILLES Treaty of and the defeat of Germany, 11

VIETNAM war in, 102

WARSAW bombed by the Germans, 21; Jews rise up against German persecution in, 80

WEST Rebecca describes Yugoslavia's resistance to Hitler, 53–54

YALTA Stalin, Roosevelt and Churchill meet at, 94, 96–97

YUGOSLAVIA accepts German demands, 52; rebels against Germany, 53; conquered by Germany, 54

ZHUKOV General Georgi drives the Germans from Moscow, 69